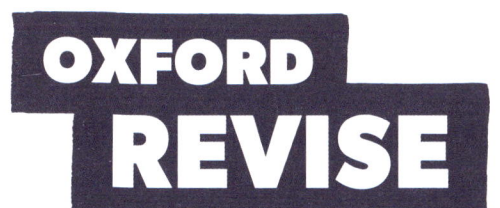

AQA GCSE

UNSEEN POETRY

English Literature

COMPLETE REVISION AND PRACTICE

Series Editor: Lyndsay Bawden

Julia Naughton

Contents

 Shade in each level of the circle as you feel more confident and ready for your exam.

How to use this book — iv

Concept knowledge 2–37

1 Introduction — 2
 - Knowledge

2 Meaning — 8
 - Knowledge
 - Retrieval

3 The poet and voice — 13
 - Knowledge
 - Retrieval

4 Poem structure — 18
 - Knowledge
 - Retrieval

5 Language — 24
 - Knowledge
 - Retrieval

Exam knowledge 38–108

6 Exam overview — 38
 - Knowledge

7 Analysing one poem — 40
 - Knowledge
 - Retrieval

8 Analysing two poems — 54
 - Knowledge
 - Retrieval

9 Example 1: analysis of one poem — 65
 - Knowledge
 - Retrieval

10 Example 1: analysis of two poems 79
- Knowledge
- Retrieval

11 Example 2: analysis of one poem 88
- Knowledge
- Retrieval

12 Example 2: analysis of two poems 98
- Knowledge
- Retrieval

Exam practice 108–115
- Practice

How to use this book

This book uses a three-step approach to revision: **Knowledge**, **Retrieval**, and **Practice**.
It is important that you do all three; they work together to make your revision effective.

 Knowledge

Knowledge comes first. Each chapter is divided into **Knowledge Organisers**. These are clear, easy-to-understand, concise summaries of the content that you need to know for your exam. The information is organised to show how one idea flows into the next so you can learn how everything is tied together.

Sample answers and examiner's comments are also provided where appropriate to help you understand what makes a good answer.

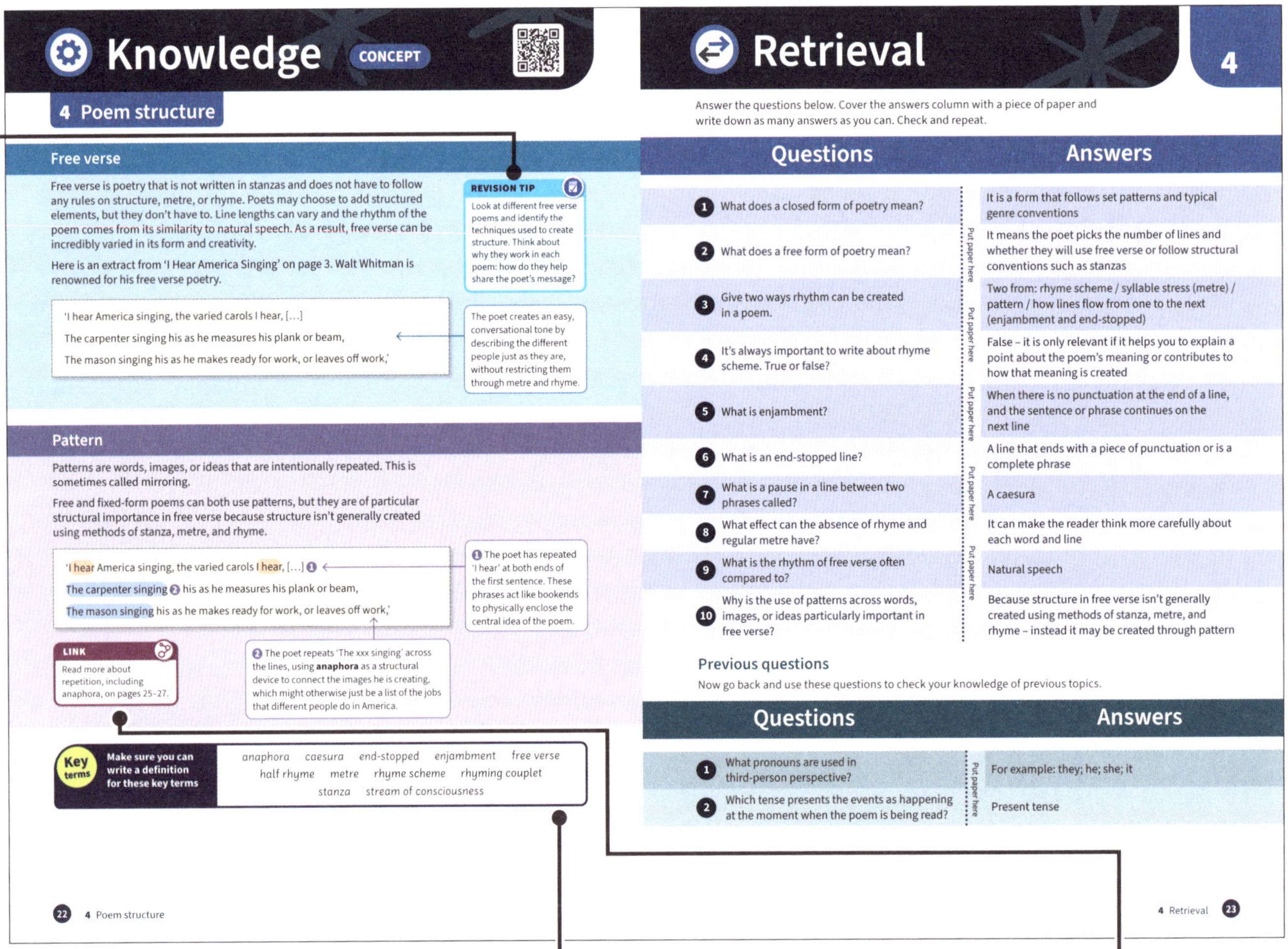

REVISION TIP

Revision tips offer you helpful advice and guidance to aid your revision and help you to understand key concepts and remember them.

REMEMBER

The **Remember** box offers useful guidance.

Key terms — Make sure you can write a definition for these key terms

The **Key terms** box highlights the key words and phrases you need to know, remember, and be able to use confidently.

LINK

The **Link** box offers a reference to a related topic or piece of knowledge that you could refer to for an exam question.

Retrieval

The **Retrieval questions** help you learn and quickly recall the information you've acquired. These are short questions and answers about the Knowledge Organiser content you have just revised. Cover up the answers with some paper and write down as many answers as you can from memory. Check back to the Knowledge Organisers for any you got wrong, then cover the answers and attempt all the questions again until you can answer *all* the questions correctly.

Make sure you revisit the Retrieval questions on different days to help them stick in your memory. You need to write down the answers each time, or say them out loud, for your revision to be effective.

Previous questions

Many Retrieval pages also have some **Retrieval questions** from **previous topics**. Answer these to see if you can remember the content from the earlier sections. If you get the answers wrong, go back and do the Retrieval questions for the earlier topics again.

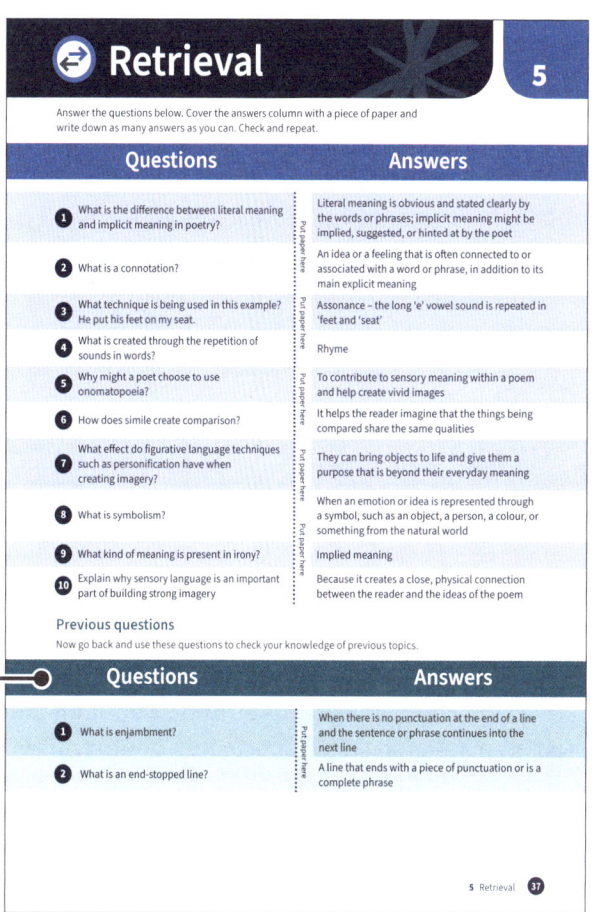

Practice

Once you are confident with the Knowledge Organisers and Retrieval questions, you can move on to the final stage: **Practice**. This can be found at the back of the book.

The **exam-style questions** in this section help you apply all the knowledge you have learned.

EXAM TIP

Exam tips show you how to interpret the questions, provide guidance on how to answer them, and give advice on how to secure as many marks as possible. Guidance is also offered on how to approach different command words.

Answers and Glossary

You can scan the QR codes at any time to access sample answers and mark schemes for the exam-style questions, a glossary containing definitions of the key terms, as well as further revision support, or go.oup.com/OR/GCSE/A/EngLit/Unseen

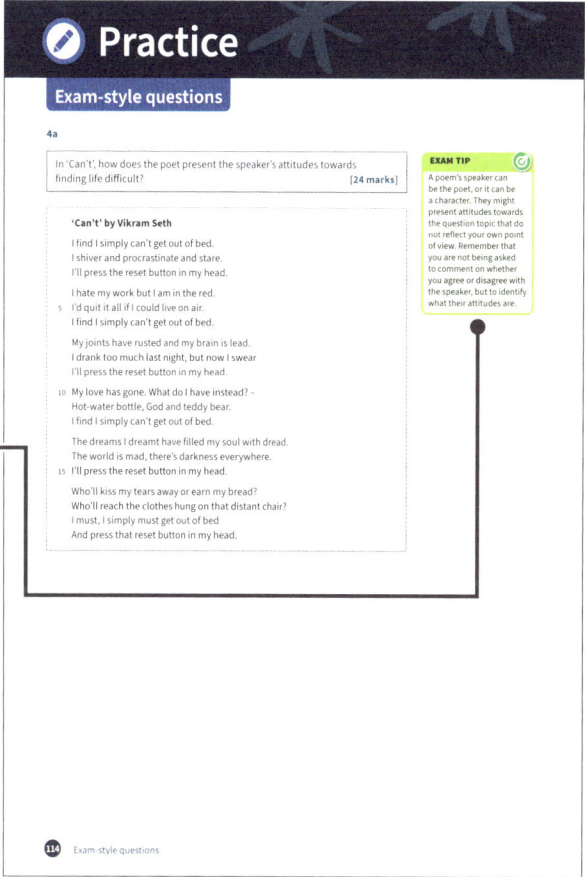

Knowledge CONCEPT

1 Introduction

Revising for the Unseen Poetry questions

Chapters 2 to 5 of this book will help you revise the concept knowledge you need for analysing unseen poems. Chapters 6 to 12 give you key information about the exam, and explore in depth the two types of questions you will encounter in the exam and how to approach these. The final Practice section gives you exam-style questions to practise the knowledge and skills you have learned.

Sample poems for analysis

Chapters 2 to 5 use extracts from five poems, which are shown here in full for you to refer to and enjoy. These poems were chosen because, together, they demonstrate a wide variety of poetic techniques.

'My Brilliant Image'

By Hafiz, this poem explores ideas about divine love and wisdom. It was written in Persia in the fourteenth century. This is a modern translation.

'There Will Come Soft Rains'

This poem, by Sara Teasdale, explores the destructive nature of war and questions humankind's place on earth. It was written during the First World War and the Flu pandemic of 1918.

'I Hear America Singing'

This poem by Walt Whitman, first published in 1860, is about how different people in America contribute to society through their work.

'London Snow'

This poem by Robert Bridges, is about an unexpected, heavy snowfall on the city of London in 1890.

'The Highwayman'

This is a gothic-style poem about a secret love affair between a highway robber and a young woman called Bess. It was written by Alfred Noyes in 1906, but is set in the 1800s.

1

REVISION TIP

Poems in the exam may contain words you don't know. Practise trying to work out the meanings of unfamiliar words yourself. The ideas in the poem and surrounding words will give clues to their meaning.

'My Brilliant Image' by Hafiz (translated by Daniel Ladinsky)

One day the sun admitted,
I am just a shadow.
I wish I could show you
The Infinite Incandescence
5 That has cast my brilliant image!

I wish I could show you,
When you are lonely or in darkness,
The Astonishing Light
Of your own Being!

'There Will Come Soft Rains' by Sara Teasdale

There will come soft rains and the smell of the ground,
And swallows circling with their shimmering sound;

And frogs in the pools singing at night,
And wild plum trees in tremulous white,

5 Robins will wear their feathery fire
Whistling their whims on a low fence-wire;

And not one will know of the war, not one
Will care at last when it is done.

Not one would mind, neither bird nor tree
10 If mankind perished utterly;

And Spring herself, when she woke at dawn,
Would scarcely know that we were gone.

tremulous: *shaky*

'I Hear America Singing' by Walt Whitman

I hear America singing, the varied carols I hear,
Those of mechanics, each one singing his as it should be blithe and strong,
The carpenter singing his as he measures his plank or beam,
The mason singing his as he makes ready for work, or leaves off work,
5 The boatman singing what belongs to him in his boat, the deckhand singing on the steamboat deck,
The shoemaker singing as he sits on his bench, the hatter singing as he stands,
The wood-cutter's song, the ploughboy's on his way in the morning, or at noon intermission or at sundown,
10 The delicious singing of the mother, or of the young wife at work, or of the girl sewing or washing,
Each singing what belongs to him or her and to none else,
The day what belongs to the day—at night the party of young fellows, robust, friendly,
15 Singing with open mouths their strong melodious songs.

deckhand: *person who works on the deck of a ship*

Knowledge CONCEPT

1 Introduction

'London Snow' by Robert Bridges

When men were all asleep the snow came flying,
In large white flakes falling on the city brown,
Stealthily and perpetually settling and loosely lying,
    Hushing the latest traffic of the drowsy town;
5 Deadening, muffling, stifling its murmurs failing;
Lazily and incessantly floating down and down:
    Silently sifting and veiling road, roof and railing;
Hiding difference, making unevenness even,
Into angles and crevices softly drifting and sailing.
10   All night it fell, and when full inches seven
It lay in the depth of its uncompacted lightness,
The clouds blew off from a high and frosty heaven;
    And all woke earlier for the unaccustomed brightness
Of the winter dawning, the strange unheavenly glare:
15 The eye marvelled—marvelled at the dazzling whiteness;
    The ear hearkened to the stillness of the solemn air;
No sound of wheel rumbling nor of foot falling,
And the busy morning cries came thin and spare.
    Then boys I heard, as they went to school, calling,
20 They gathered up the crystal manna to freeze
Their tongues with tasting, their hands with snowballing;
    Or rioted in a drift, plunging up to the knees;
Or peering up from under the white-mossed wonder,
'O look at the trees!' they cried, 'O look at the trees!'
25   With lessened load a few carts creak and blunder,
Following along the white deserted way,
A country company long dispersed asunder:
    When now already the sun, in pale display
Standing by Paul's high dome, spread forth below
30 His sparkling beams, and awoke the stir of the day.
    For now doors open, and war is waged with the snow;
And trains of sombre men, past tale of number,
Tread long brown paths, as toward their toil they go:
    But even for them awhile no cares encumber
35 Their minds diverted; the daily word is unspoken,
The daily thoughts of labour and sorrow slumber
At the sight of the beauty that greets them, for the charm they have broken.

hearkened: *listened*   **asunder:** *apart*
manna: *God-given food in the Bible*

'The Highwayman' by Alfred Noyes

PART ONE

The wind was a torrent of darkness among the gusty trees.
The moon was a ghostly galleon tossed upon cloudy seas.
The road was a ribbon of moonlight over the purple moor,
And the highwayman came riding—
5   Riding—riding—
The highwayman came riding, up to the old inn-door.

He'd a French cocked-hat on his forehead, a bunch of lace at his chin,
A coat of the claret velvet, and breeches of brown doe-skin.
They fitted with never a wrinkle. His boots were up to the thigh.
10 And he rode with a jewelled twinkle,
    His pistol butts a-twinkle,
His rapier hilt a-twinkle, under the jewelled sky.

Over the cobbles he clattered and clashed in the dark inn-yard.
He tapped with his whip on the shutters, but all was locked and barred.
15 He whistled a tune to the window, and who should be waiting there
But the landlord's black-eyed daughter,
    Bess, the landlord's daughter,
Plaiting a dark red love-knot into her long black hair.

And dark in the dark old inn-yard a stable-wicket creaked
20 Where Tim the ostler listened. His face was white and peaked.
His eyes were hollows of madness, his hair like mouldy hay,
But he loved the landlord's daughter,
    The landlord's red-lipped daughter.
Dumb as a dog he listened, and he heard the robber say—

25 "One kiss, my bonny sweetheart, I'm after a prize to-night,
But I shall be back with the yellow gold before the morning light;
Yet, if they press me sharply, and harry me through the day,
Then look for me by moonlight,
    Watch for me by moonlight,
30 I'll come to thee by moonlight, though hell should bar the way."

He rose upright in the stirrups. He scarce could reach her hand,
But she loosened her hair in the casement. His face burnt like a brand
As the black cascade of perfume came tumbling over his breast;
And he kissed its waves in the moonlight,
35   (O, sweet black waves in the moonlight!)
Then he tugged at his rein in the moonlight, and galloped away to the west.

continued

PART TWO

He did not come in the dawning. He did not come at noon;
And out of the tawny sunset, before the rise of the moon,
When the road was a gypsy's ribbon, looping the purple moor,
40 A red-coat troop came marching—
    Marching—marching—
King George's men came marching, up to the old inn-door.

They said no word to the landlord. They drank his ale instead.
But they gagged his daughter, and bound her, to the foot of her narrow bed.
45 Two of them knelt at her casement, with muskets at their side!
There was death at every window;
    And hell at one dark window;
For Bess could see, through her casement, the road that he would ride.

They had tied her up to attention, with many a sniggering jest.
50 They had bound a musket beside her, with the muzzle beneath her breast!
"Now, keep good watch!" and they kissed her. She heard the doomed man
    say—
Look for me by moonlight;
    Watch for me by moonlight;
55 I'll come to thee by moonlight, though hell should bar the way!

She twisted her hands behind her; but all the knots held good!
She writhed her hands till her fingers were wet with sweat or blood!
They stretched and strained in the darkness, and the hours crawled by like
    years
60 Till, now, on the stroke of midnight,
    Cold, on the stroke of midnight,
The tip of one finger touched it! The trigger at least was hers!

The tip of one finger touched it. She strove no more for the rest.
Up, she stood up to attention, with the muzzle beneath her breast.
65 She would not risk their hearing; she would not strive again;
For the road lay bare in the moonlight;
    Blank and bare in the moonlight;
And the blood of her veins, in the moonlight, throbbed to her love's refrain.

Tlot-tlot; tlot-tlot! Had they heard it? The horsehoofs ringing clear;
70 Tlot-tlot; tlot-tlot, in the distance? Were they deaf that they did not hear?
Down the ribbon of moonlight, over the brow of the hill,
The highwayman came riding—
    Riding—riding—
The red coats looked to their priming! She stood up, straight and still.

continued

75   Tlot-tlot, in the frosty silence! Tlot-tlot, in the echoing night!
     Nearer he came and nearer. Her face was like a light.
     Her eyes grew wide for a moment; she drew one last deep breath,
     Then her finger moved in the moonlight,
        Her musket shattered the moonlight,
80   Shattered her breast in the moonlight and warned him—with her death.

     He turned. He spurred to the west; he did not know who stood
     Bowed, with her head o'er the musket, drenched with her own blood!
     Not till the dawn he heard it, and his face grew grey to hear
     How Bess, the landlord's daughter,
85   The landlord's black-eyed daughter,
     Had watched for her love in the moonlight, and died in the darkness there.

     Back, he spurred like a madman, shrieking a curse to the sky,
     With the white road smoking behind him and his rapier brandished high.
     Blood red were his spurs in the golden noon; wine-red was his velvet coat;
90   When they shot him down on the highway,
        Down like a dog on the highway,
     And he lay in his blood on the highway, with a bunch of lace at his throat.

         . . .

     And still of a winter's night, they say, when the wind is in the trees,
     When the moon is a ghostly galleon tossed upon cloudy seas,
95   When the road is a ribbon of moonlight over the purple moor,
     A highwayman comes riding—
        Riding—riding—
     A highwayman comes riding, up to the old inn-door.

     Over the cobbles he clatters and clangs in the dark inn-yard.
100 He taps with his whip on the shutters, but all is locked and barred.
     He whistles a tune to the window, and who should be waiting there
     But the landlord's black-eyed daughter,
        Bess, the landlord's daughter,
     Plaiting a dark red love-knot into her long black hair.

butts: *handles*
rapier hilt: *sword handle*
wicket: *gate*
ostler: *person who looks after the horses*
harry: *trouble or bother*

thee: *you*
casement: *window*
brand: *clear shape*
muzzle: *the open end of a gun*

Knowledge CONCEPT

2 Meaning

Understanding and responding to meaning

This section focuses on some of the broader decisions a poet makes. Most poets have clear intentions and messages to share in their poems. However, the emotional response of the reader is a key part of a poem's success. As a result, different readers may find different meanings, and there can be many pockets of meaning within a whole poem.

In the exam, you are not expected to try to understand every single meaning in a poem. Instead, you must show you understand the poem's meaning *in connection to the question focus*. Part of this is identifying what the poet is saying (and how they say it), and part of this is your own personal response to that.

> **REVISION TIP**
>
> All the knowledge covered in this section will help you revise the tools a poet uses to create meaning.

What is the poem about?

The first thing to establish is what the poem is literally about: a flower, a father, the ocean, missing the school bus, for example. Some poems may build their meaning very simply from this, for example, to show the beauty of a favourite flower as it opens, or how a younger brother always misses the bus. You must understand what the poem is about in order to work out how the poet develops that to create much deeper meanings.

Literal meanings of the sample poems in Chapter 1

Poem	What it is about
'My Brilliant Image'	The sun talking
'There Will Come Soft Rains'	The natural world and war
'I Hear America Singing'	Different people in America
'London Snow'	A snowfall
'The Highwayman'	A highway robber and his girlfriend

Theme

The **theme** of a poem is the core idea or message that the poet wants to share, such as love, hate, desire, illness, war, peace, beauty, growing up, or sadness. There may be clues to the theme in the title of the poem, or it may be something you need to work out across the whole poem from its content.

The exam question may reference the theme or direct you to a general area to focus on, from which you can begin to work out both the theme and the poet's **attitude** towards it.

Theme is just one part of a poem's overall meaning: poems can contain several layers of ideas to explore, or they can cover more than one theme.

Extract from 'The Highwayman'

'And he kissed ❶ its waves in the moonlight'

'Two of them knelt at her casement, with muskets ❷ at their side!'

LINK
See examples of how the exam questions will be worded on page 39.

❶ One key theme of 'The Highwayman' is love: the highwayman loves Bess, she loves him, and the ostler has an unrequited love for Bess.

❷ A second key theme in the poem is violence: the highwayman is a violent robber, the soldiers come to shoot him, and Bess shoots herself.

Context

Context has two meanings:

- The time, place, and situation in which the poem was written
- The world of the poem itself

The only context that is important is the general understanding about the world that you bring to the poem and the information you can find within it. You need to think about the meaning of the poem in connection to the world that you know and understand.

You will *not* be given any information about the time, place, and situation in which the poem was written, therefore you will not be expected to write about this.

Extract from 'The Highwayman'

'One kiss, my bonny sweetheart, I'm after a prize to-night,

But I shall be back with the yellow gold before the morning light;

Yet, if they press me sharply, and harry me through the day'

You might know that highwaymen violently robbed coaches. This context is reflected in the language used between the lovers. The poet uses this **context** to help build the idea that Bess's love for the highwayman is dangerous and will lead them both to a violent end.

2 Knowledge

Knowledge CONCEPT

2 Meaning

Allusion

Allusion refers to the brief references a poet might include in their poem, such as to other literary works, historical events, mythical or philosophical ideas, and well-known people or places. Allusion is connected to context because identifying and understanding these references can allow the reader to:

- understand the poem more deeply
- access a new meaning in the poem
- make connections between ideas in different poems or pieces of literature.

Extract from 'London Snow'

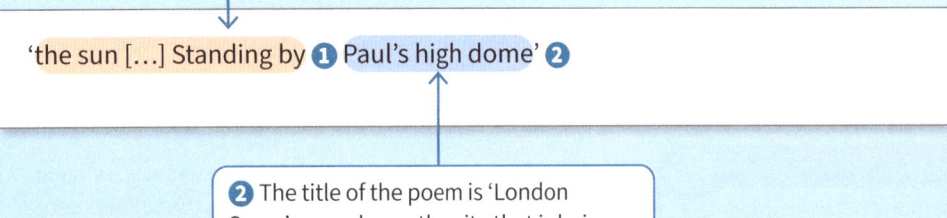

'the sun [...] Standing by ❶ Paul's high dome' ❷

❶ The position of the sun beside the high cathedral roof physically connects the sun to the church. This could mean the poet wants to say something about religion or God by showing the way the sun reaches down and touches the snow with its light.

❷ The title of the poem is 'London Snow', so we know the city that is being described; the poet then alludes to St Paul's cathedral here – a large church with a famous domed roof.

Genre

The **genre** of a poem is the poetic category into which it falls – but remember that not every poem fits into a neat genre. Genres have typical conventions (rules and techniques) which can direct the **form** of the poem, the style of language it uses, or the type of content.

LINK
Read more about form and the physical construction of poems in Chapter 4 on pages 18–23.

Common poetic genres

Genre	Description	Example
acrostic	A poem where the first letter of each line together spells out a word or message	'Elizabeth' by Edgar Allen Poe
allegory	A poem where the main characters and events represent other characters, events, or ideas to create meaning. Allegories often draw on history, religion, or morality, and act as a long, **extended metaphor**.	'Inferno: Canto I' by Dante (Dante goes on a journey – this symbolises the journey to hell)
ballad	A song-like poem which tells a story, often in a traditional folk style	'The Highwayman' by Alfred Noyes
dramatic monologue	A poem from the point of view of one speaker which reveals their private thoughts and feelings	'Mrs Midas' by Carol Ann Duffy

Genre	Description	Example
elegy	A poem that reflects on a death, and often involves grief and praise, and then ends with consolation	'In Memoriam A. H. H.' by Alfred, Lord Tennyson
epic	A long poem that retells the events of a heroic individual's life, or an important historic event	'Omeros' by Derek Walcott
fable	A poem that includes talking animals or objects, which usually includes a strong moral lesson	'Fable' by Ralph Waldo Emerson
lament	A poem expressing grief or loss	'Stop All the Clocks' by W.H. Auden
narrative	A poem that tells a story or recounts an event; it often includes the voice of a **narrator** as well as characters. Other poems, such as ballads, are also narratives.	'London Snow' by Robert Bridges
ode or lyric	A poem that reveals the personal emotions of the poet towards a particular subject, but briefly; usually written in the first person and using stanzas. Traditionally, these poems could be sung.	'Y cynta' I weld y môr' (Seeing the Sea) by Menna Elfyn
parody	A poem written to imitate another poet or poem's style and poke fun at it. It is usually funny but may also have a message to share.	'Twinkle Twinkle Little Bat' by Lewis Carroll
pastoral	A poem written to idealise the countryside and the rural way of life	'The Passionate Shepherd to His Love' by Christopher Marlowe
pattern or shaped	A pattern poem (or shaped verse) is where the lines of a poem are physically shaped on the page in a particular **image** or pattern to help **convey** meaning and emotional connection.	'The Mouse's Tail' by Lewis Carroll
sonnet	A poem of 14 long lines, where each line typically has 10 syllables and every other syllable is emphasised. Traditionally about love, but modern sonnets may explore different themes	'Love is Not All' (Sonnet XXX) by Edna St Vincent Millay
satire	A poem that makes a moral **judgement** by mocking the subject of the poem	'Anthem For Doomed Youth' by Wilfred Owen

> **REVISION TIP**
> You do not have to identify the type of poem the writer has used but, if you do, you should link it to how the style or form used affects the meaning in some way.

Key terms — Make sure you can write a definition for these key terms

allusion attitude context convey extended metaphor
form genre image judgement narrator theme

Retrieval

Answer the questions below. Cover the answers column with a piece of paper and write down as many answers as you can. Check and repeat.

Questions / Answers

1. In the exam, you must try to find every possible meaning in a poem. True or false?
   — False

2. Why is understanding the poem's literal meaning useful?
   — When you understand what the poem is about, you can then work out how the poet develops that to create much deeper meanings

3. What is meant by the theme of a poem?
   — The core idea or message that the poet wants to share

4. Give two examples of possible themes for a poem.
   — Two from: love / hate / desire / illness / war / peace / beauty / growing up / sadness

5. What sort of general understanding of your own might you use in analysing a poem?
   — A general understanding about the world

6. Which of these shows allusion?
   a) 'Tik Tok Tik Tok goes the teenage clock.'
   b) 'O, my brother Bob is a beautiful boy.'
   — a) 'Tik Tok Tik Tok goes the teenage clock'; because it refers to the well-known social media platform, while 'Bob' is an unknown figure

7. What is a satire?
   — A poem that makes a moral judgement by mocking the subject of the poem

8. What does 'convention' mean in poetry?
   — A set of rules or techniques in a genre

9. All poems fit into at least one genre. True or false?
   — False – some poems do not fit any particular genre

10. What is a ballad?
    — A song-like poem which tells a story, often in a traditional folk style

11. Which two genres of poetry would typically express grief or loss?
    — Lament; elegy

12. Which genre of poetry tells a story or recounts an event?
    — Narrative

12 2 Meaning

Knowledge

CONCEPT

3 The poet and voice

Analysing voice, perspective, and atmosphere

The poet plays a part in the poem, even if they aren't a character in the poem's story. The poet directs and controls the poem's **perspective** and therefore influences how a reader feels and responds to the content. Recognising the **voice** and the point of view, as well as the **atmosphere** being created, will help you understand the poem's message.

Title and poet

Always read the poem title and the poet's name first. Some poems have vague or mysterious titles, but many give clear clues as to their content and/or the poet's attitude, such as 'To my Dear and Loving Husband'.

The poet's name may give you additional information, if you happen to have read other poems by them, such as about their usual style or the common themes they explore.

Voice

The voice, or speaker, of the poem may not be the poet and so we often talk about the voice as though they and the poet are separate things. The voice is something that is created as part of the poet's craft.

The voice may be a human character, an animal, or even an inanimate object, such as a postbox. It could also be something from the natural world, such as a waterfall.

> **REVISION TIP**
> Look out for words that are intended to create a feeling in the reader, such as **pathos**.

Ask yourself questions like these about the voice:

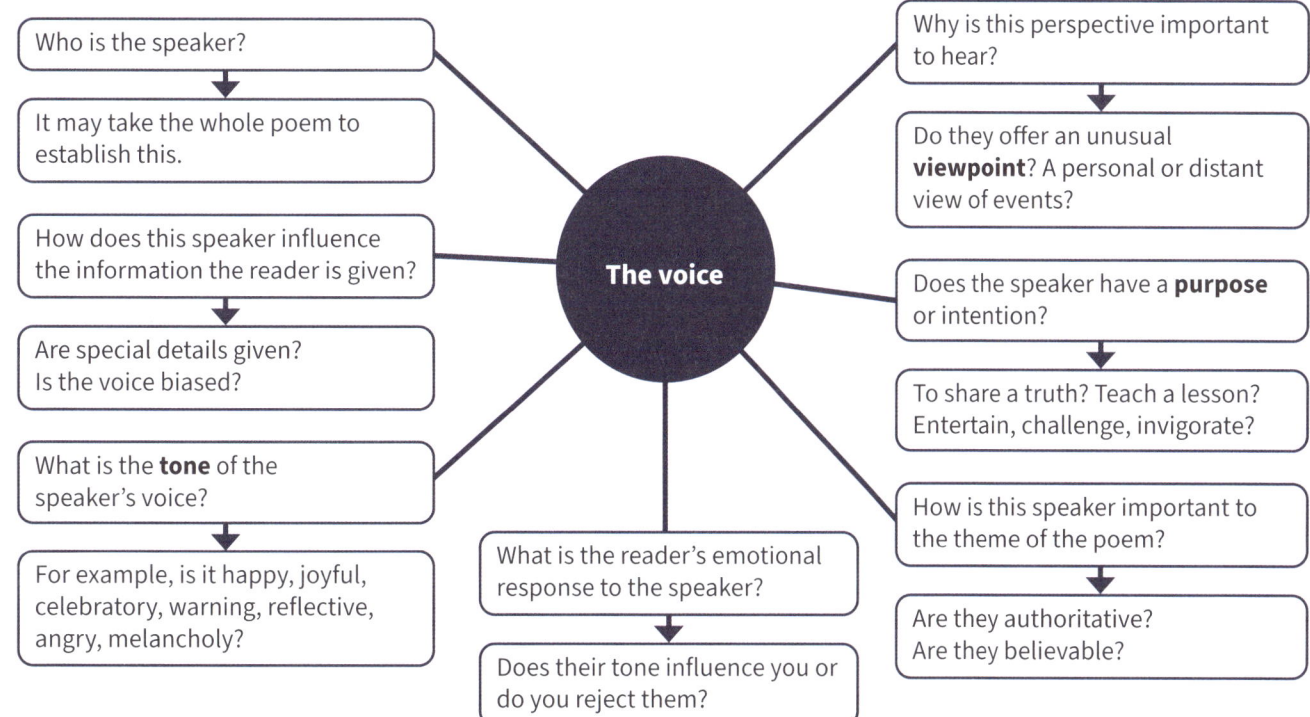

Knowledge — CONCEPT

3 The poet and voice

Using perspective to craft voice

The voice of the poem may use a single perspective such as first person, second person, or third person, or combine more than one perspective in different stanzas or lines.

First-person perspective

This is written from the point of view of the speaker, using personal pronouns and possessives such as: I, my, we, our.

> 'Then boys I heard, as they went to school, calling'

By writing in the first person, events are retold from one point of view and the poet allows the reader to share the speaker's personal experience.

Second-person perspective

This is written to draw the reader into the poem. It directs the events of the poem towards the reader, or invites them to participate in them, using the personal pronouns and possessives: you, yours.

It can be used where the poem is written to speak to a particular person imagined to be the reader, such as a lover, a parent, or child.

> 'I wish I could show you,
> When you are lonely or in darkness,
> The Astonishing Light
> Of your own Being!'

*By writing directly to the reader in 'My Brilliant Image', a more personal connection is made between the poet and **audience**. Second-person perspective can create an intimate or confiding tone.*

Third-person perspective

This is written from the point of view of someone outside the events of the poem, using personal pronouns such as: they, he, she, it.

> 'Her eyes grew wide for a moment; she drew one last deep breath'

By writing in the third person in 'The Highwayman', events are presented from an objective viewpoint, allowing more than one point of view to be shared and for the reader to understand the thoughts and feelings of multiple characters.

> **REMEMBER**
>
> If the perspective changes in a poem, ask yourself why the poet has done this. Also, think about how it makes you feel. You are expected to comment on the **methods** a poet uses, but also the personal response this creates in you. For example: does it draw you into the poem, or push you away to view events more objectively?

How tense contributes to voice

Past tense

Past tense allows the voice to recount events that have already happened.

This example is from 'London Snow':

> 'When men were all asleep the snow came flying'

Using the past tense can have a 'storytelling' effect on the poem: the reader is set at a distance from the events that have already taken place.

Present tense

Present tense allows the voice to describe events that are unfolding during the poem.

This example is from 'London Snow':

> 'For now doors open, and war is waged with the snow;
> And trains of sombre men, past tale of number,
> Tread long brown paths, as toward their toil they go'

Using the present tense engages the reader more actively because it presents the events as happening right at the moment the poem is being read.

Future tense

Future tense allows the voice to imagine events that have not yet happened but that might.

This example is from 'There Will Come Soft Rains':

> 'There will come soft rains and the smell of the ground'

Using the future tense can create a feeling of hope as future possibilities are explored. This may be used as a **contrast** to events presented in the present or past tense elsewhere in a poem.

> **REVISION TIP**
> Look for changes of tense and identify the effect these have. Both 'London Snow' and 'The Highwayman' begin in the past tense and finish in the present tense. This draws the reader in to become an active participant in the events, rather than a passive observer of the past.

> **REMEMBER**
> Consider whether tense is being used to build the poet's tone. Past tense is particularly useful for recounting memories, which may add to a tone of nostalgia or regret. Poems can also use a combination of tenses.

Attitude

The attitude or viewpoint of a speaker is shown through the thoughts and ideas they express within the poem. The ways they present them also reveal their viewpoint. These can include many different **figurative language** techniques such as **repetition** and emotional vocabulary, and structural techniques such as isolating key lines or use of dramatic monologue. Together, these things create the speaker's tone.

> 'Her face was like a light.
> Her eyes grew wide for a moment; she drew one last deep breath'

'The Highwayman' tells the story of doomed love between the highwayman and Bess. The speaker's viewpoint is sympathetic towards the main characters. This is shown through the romantic tone of the poem and the dramatic way Bess's death is presented as self-sacrifice.

Knowledge — CONCEPT

3 The poet and voice

Atmosphere and mood

Atmosphere is the general feeling created within a poem. A poem's **mood** comes from how the reader responds to and **interprets** the tone and atmosphere: essentially, how the reader feels.

'Hushing the latest traffic ❶ of the drowsy ❶ town;
Deadening, muffling, stifling its murmurs failing ❷;
Lazily and incessantly floating ❷ down and down:' ❸

❶ The atmosphere created within the poem is quiet and sleepy.

❷ The tone of the poet in 'London Snow' shows the snow as something gentle yet powerful, as it can make a whole city quiet.

❸ The mood the reader feels at this point of the poem is peace, tranquillity, and perhaps wonder.

Emotion

There can be more than one emotion presented within a poem, either because there are multiple characters and viewpoints within it, or because the speaker may share different emotions at different moments. Identifying the emotions of the speaker helps you to understand their viewpoint more clearly and to be more precise in explaining what the poem is trying to say.

'His boots were up to the thigh.
And he rode with a jewelled twinkle'

In 'The Highwayman', the speaker shows admiration for the highwayman, even though he is a villain, because he is bold, well-dressed, and daring.

'Where Tim the ostler listened. His face was white and peaked.
His eyes were hollows of madness, his hair like mouldy hay'

The speaker shows distaste for Bess's other admirer, who hides in the shadows, and suggests he is pale, unhinged, and rotten. Presenting different emotions gives the poem's story greater depth and creates contrast to evoke specific emotional responses in the reader.

Key terms — Make sure you can write a definition for these key terms

atmosphere   audience   contrast   figurative language   interpret
method   mood   pathos   perspective   purpose
repetition   tone   viewpoint   voice

Retrieval

Answer the questions below. Cover the answers column with a piece of paper and write down as many answers as you can. Check and repeat.

Questions / Answers

#	Question	Answer
1	Why should you always read the title of the poem?	Because it might give clear clues as to the poem's content and/or the poet's attitude
2	The poet and the voice of the poem are the same thing. True or false?	False – poems are written either from the poet's perspective or from the perspective of a 'character' in the poem, so the voice, or speaker, of the poem may not be the poet
3	What is the effect of writing in first-person perspective?	Events are told from one point of view and the reader shares the speaker's experience
4	What is the effect of writing in second-person perspective?	Writing directly to the reader creates a more personal connection between poet and reader
5	What pronouns are used in third-person perspective?	For example: they; he; she; it
6	Which tense can have a 'storytelling' effect and set the reader at a distance from events that have already happened?	Past tense
7	Which tense presents the events as happening at the moment when the poem is being read?	Present tense
8	How is the viewpoint of a poet shown in a poem?	Through the thoughts and ideas they express and in the ways they present them
9	What is the difference between atmosphere and mood?	Atmosphere is the general feeling within a poem; mood comes from how the reader responds to and interprets the poem
10	What effect do contrasting emotions in a poem have on the story within it?	Presenting different emotions allows the story of the poem to have greater depth

Previous questions

Now go back and use these questions to check your knowledge of previous topics.

Questions / Answers

#	Question	Answer
1	What is meant by the theme of a poem?	The core idea or message that the poet wants to share
2	What does 'convention' mean in poetry?	A set of rules or techniques in a genre

3 Retrieval

Knowledge CONCEPT

4 Poem structure

Analysing the form and structure

The poet makes decisions about how they will physically construct the form of their poem. These decisions will complement the poem's theme or allow particular ideas or feelings to stand out.

- 'Closed' forms of poetry follow set patterns and typical genre conventions, such as sonnets, which have 14 lines.
- 'Free' forms of poetry mean the poet picks the number of lines, and chooses whether to use **free verse** or follow structural conventions, such as stanzas.

All poets create rhythm through their choices concerning **rhyme scheme**, syllable stress, pattern, and how lines flow from one to the next. Together, these decisions create the structure into which the words can flow and take life.

> **REVISION TIP**
> It will help your understanding if you can recognise how a poem has been constructed. However, only write about elements such as rhyme scheme if they help you to explain a point about the poem's meaning or contribute to how that meaning is created. Every element or method you write about must be *relevant*.

Lines

All poems have two things in common: words and lines. Poets manipulate lines to share their poem's meaning in particular ways.

Line length

A line can be as short as a single word, or longer than the width of a page. A short line has a quick, instant effect on the reader, while a longer line requires more effort and concentration from the reader to absorb all the detail. They might be compared to a photograph and a video: both share an image, but give a different impression of the image and evoke a different reaction.

> **REMEMBER**
> Remember, punctuation is an important part of rhythm in poetry because it shows the reader where to pause and where to stop.

End-stopped

A line that ends with a piece of punctuation or is a complete phrase, is called **end-stopped**. It means the thought contained in the line stops, or is paused, at the end of that line. Using end-stopped lines helps a poem have a regulated and orderly feel, which might reflect the ideas presented within it. It also allows ideas to be clearly separated.

Enjambment

This is when there is no punctuation at the end of a line and the sentence or phrase continues on to the next line. **Enjambed** lines allow ideas to flow through a poem, which can create contrasting feelings. For example, it could contribute to a more relaxed atmosphere, but if used in a **stream of consciousness**, it could create an excited, rushed, tumbling feeling.

Caesura

A **caesura** is a pause in a line between two phrases. It can occur at any point and is usually created through punctuation, such as a comma, full stop, semi-colon, colon, or dash. A caesura deliberately breaks the flow of the line and can be used for different purposes, such as to force the reader to pause, to think about what has just been said, to shift focus, or to allow a change in rhythm.

'He whistled a tune to the window, ❶ and who should be waiting there ❷
But the landlord's black-eyed daughter, ❸
Bess, the landlord's daughter,' ❹

❶ The comma creates a caesura to separate the phrases and shift the focus away from the highwayman outside the inn, to whoever is waiting for him within it.

❷ The description of who is waiting for the highwayman is enjambed over two lines to create a brief moment of suspense because the reader's eye has to skip down to the next line to find out who it is.

❸ The comma end-stops the enjambed sentence and marks the conclusion of this image. The next sentence goes on to add more detail to the image of who is waiting, but it is contained as an aside to the reader within the commas.

❹ Line 5 of every stanza in 'The Highwayman' is a short, focused line, repeating an image set out in line 4. The effect of this is to emphasise that the image is important and to fix it in the reader's mind.

Stanzas

A **stanza** is a group of lines within a poem. Stanzas have different names depending on the number of lines within them. For example:

- monostich – single-line stanza
- couplet – two-line stanza
- tercet – three-line stanza
- quatrain – four-line stanza
- quintain – five-line stanza
- sestet – six-line stanza
- septet – seven-line stanza
- octave – eight-line stanza

REVISION TIP
You do not need to identify the names of the stanza types in the exam; you can simply say 'four-line stanza', etc.

Single-line stanzas can be used in a variety of ways; for example, to draw attention to a particular image or idea, to create an echo, to act as a second voice, to slow the pace of a poem, or to create a pause.

Poets may use stanzas of different lengths for effect, sometimes repeating a stanza for a 'chorus' effect.

Poets can use stanzas to act as little 'pockets' of a poem, each one containing an idea, an image, or a moment that contributes towards the poem's meaning as a whole.

The space between stanzas might make the reader pause to think about an idea that stands out, or it might create meaning (e.g. a space between two people arguing could build the idea that they disagree or are alienated).

Knowledge CONCEPT

4 Poem structure

Look at the poems on pages 3–7.
- 'My Brilliant Image' is written in two stanzas of uneven length.
- 'There Will Come Soft Rains' is written in couplets.
- 'I Hear America Singing' and 'London Snow' are written as single stanzas. ❶
- 'The Highwayman' is written in six-line stanzas, divided into two parts. ❷

❶ 'London Snow' describes a particular event (the snowfall) as it happens over a single night and morning. Writing in a single stream of description allows the poet to mirror the action of the snow itself, which falls heavily and without a break all night.

❷ 'The Highwayman' is a ballad. It tells a dramatic story rather like a play does, so the regular stanzas and the two-part structure help shift the focus of the story like a change of Act or scene.

Rhythm

The starting point of a poem's rhythm is usually its **metre** and how the poet uses rhyme.

Metre

A poet chooses a metre that will allow particular words or syllables to be emphasised. This focuses the reader on those words, and consequently, on the ideas of the poem. It also contributes to the rhythm of the poem.

Rhythm may be regular and help carry the reader along, or it may be irregular and create pauses or hesitations, and therefore make a poem feel more like a conversation. Irregular metre can make a poem more challenging to read – but this is done deliberately by the poet and therefore you must ask yourself what purpose it serves.

> **REMEMBER**
> Metre is the rhythmic structure of a line or a group of lines – the beat of the poem. When the line is read out, the words or syllables that are stressed or emphasised create the rhythmic beats.

Rhyme

Rhyme is where two or more words share an exact sound, such as *night* and *light* (full rhyme) or a similar sound, such as *good* and *blood* (**half rhyme**). It is not essential in a poem and it can occur at any point – it will not always be at the ends of lines. Words within the same line may rhyme, and if a poet chooses to do this it will build rhythm into the poem in a different way.

Rhyme scheme

The rhyme scheme is the pattern of rhyme that occurs within a stanza or set of lines, and across the whole poem.

- A regular rhyme scheme such as ABAB means the end of alternate lines will rhyme.
- An irregular rhyme scheme such as ABCA CBDEA will mean there is no set repetition in the pattern of rhyme.

Look at the poems on pages 3–7.

- 'My Brilliant Image' is written without using rhyme or a regular metre. ❶
- 'There Will Come Soft Rains' is written in **rhyming couplets** with a rhyme scheme AA BB CC DD EE FF. The metre is the same within the lines of each separate couplet, except for lines 8 and 12, which are shorter than lines 9 and 11 and have matching metre – both are also end-stopped lines.
- 'London Snow' might look like free verse because it is only one stanza, but it uses a regular rhyme scheme across sections of nine lines: ABABCBCDC, with a final line adding an extra D rhyme. ❷
- 'I Hear America Singing' is written without using rhyme or a regular metre.
- 'The Highwayman' has a regular rhyme scheme AABCCB within each stanza. Line 5 of each stanza is a partial repetition of line 4, and sometimes line 6 repeats or extends the image created in lines 4 and 5.

❶ The absence of rhyme and regular metre could be seen to make the reader think more carefully about each word and line in this poem. They cannot rely on a rhythm or rules to carry them along, which suggests this poet wants you to think only about the lesson they are trying to teach.

❷ The poet has chosen to use a complex but regular rhyme scheme. This could be seen to reflect the rhythmic nature of the snow and how it behaves – not chaotically (as unrhyming free verse could be) but in an orderly, calm manner, having a soothing effect on the world below.

REVISION TIP

Some forms of poetry have formal rules, for example sonnets have 14 lines, a regular rhyme scheme, and a regular metre. Shakespeare used a rhyme scheme of ABABCDCDEFEFGG in his sonnets, and iambic pentameter, which means 10 beats in a line. But be careful – poets love to break rules and some modern sonnets do not obey the rules on rhyme or metre and simply have 14 lines.

Knowledge CONCEPT

4 Poem structure

Free verse

Free verse is poetry that is not written in stanzas and does not have to follow any rules on structure, metre, or rhyme. Poets may choose to add structured elements, but they don't have to. Line lengths can vary and the rhythm of the poem comes from its similarity to natural speech. As a result, free verse can be incredibly varied in its form and creativity.

Here is an extract from 'I Hear America Singing' on page 3. Walt Whitman is renowned for his free verse poetry.

> 'I hear America singing, the varied carols I hear, […]
> The carpenter singing his as he measures his plank or beam,
> The mason singing his as he makes ready for work, or leaves off work,'

REVISION TIP

Look at different free verse poems and identify the techniques used to create structure. Think about why they work in each poem: how do they help share the poet's message?

The poet creates an easy, conversational tone by describing the different people just as they are, without restricting them through metre and rhyme.

Pattern

Patterns are words, images, or ideas that are intentionally repeated. This is sometimes called mirroring.

Free and fixed-form poems can both use patterns, but they are of particular structural importance in free verse because structure isn't generally created using methods of stanza, metre, and rhyme.

> 'I hear America singing, the varied carols I hear, […] ❶
> The carpenter singing ❷ his as he measures his plank or beam,
> The mason singing his as he makes ready for work, or leaves off work,'

❶ The poet has repeated 'I hear' at both ends of the first sentence. These phrases act like bookends to physically enclose the central idea of the poem.

LINK
Read more about repetition, including anaphora, on pages 25–27.

❷ The poet repeats 'The xxx singing' across the lines, using **anaphora** as a structural device to connect the images he is creating, which might otherwise just be a list of the jobs that different people do in America.

 **Key terms** Make sure you can write a definition for these key terms

anaphora   caesura   end-stopped   enjambment   free verse
half rhyme   metre   rhyme scheme   rhyming couplet
stanza   stream of consciousness

Retrieval

Answer the questions below. Cover the answers column with a piece of paper and write down as many answers as you can. Check and repeat.

Questions / Answers

#	Question	Answer
1	What does a closed form of poetry mean?	It is a form that follows set patterns and typical genre conventions
2	What does a free form of poetry mean?	It means the poet picks the number of lines and whether they will use free verse or follow structural conventions such as stanzas
3	Give two ways rhythm can be created in a poem.	Two from: rhyme scheme / syllable stress (metre) / pattern / how lines flow from one to the next (enjambment and end-stopped)
4	It's always important to write about rhyme scheme. True or false?	False – it is only relevant if it helps you to explain a point about the poem's meaning or contributes to how that meaning is created
5	What is enjambment?	When there is no punctuation at the end of a line, and the sentence or phrase continues on the next line
6	What is an end-stopped line?	A line that ends with a piece of punctuation or is a complete phrase
7	What is a pause in a line between two phrases called?	A caesura
8	What effect can the absence of rhyme and regular metre have?	It can make the reader think more carefully about each word and line
9	What is the rhythm of free verse often compared to?	Natural speech
10	Why is the use of patterns across words, images, or ideas particularly important in free verse?	Because structure in free verse isn't generally created using methods of stanza, metre, and rhyme – instead it may be created through pattern

Previous questions

Now go back and use these questions to check your knowledge of previous topics.

Questions / Answers

#	Question	Answer
1	What pronouns are used in third-person perspective?	For example: they; he; she; it
2	Which tense presents the events as happening at the moment when the poem is being read?	Present tense

Knowledge — CONCEPT

5 Language

Identifying meaning

Analysing the language

Understanding and analysing the language of poetry is an essential part of the Unseen Poetry exam.

- As part of Question 27.1, you might want to write about the writer's choice of words to unpick the meaning of the poem. You will need to explain your personal response and your interpretations by using textual references. You will also need to identify and **analyse** the language choices the poet has made and how those create meaning and effect.
- As part of Question 27.2, you could identify the language choices a second poet has made in their poem, comment on their effects, and compare the methods with the first poet's choices.

The first step in language analysis is to understand how meaning can be layered in a poem. Poets choose words not only for their literal meanings, but for what they suggest and the images they create.

Literal (explicit) meaning

The **explicit** meaning is obvious and stated clearly by the words or phrases in the poem. It does not need deep thought or interpretation.

> 'When men were all asleep the snow came flying'

In this extract from 'London Snow', the literal meaning is that it snowed while everyone was asleep.

Inferred (implicit) meaning

Implicit meanings are not obvious but must be worked out. There may be clues, such as a word choice that has multiple meanings, or the positioning of particular words together.

Use the information in the poem to work out what the poet is implying, suggesting, or hinting. There may be more than one possible **inferred** meaning, as in this example from 'London Snow'.

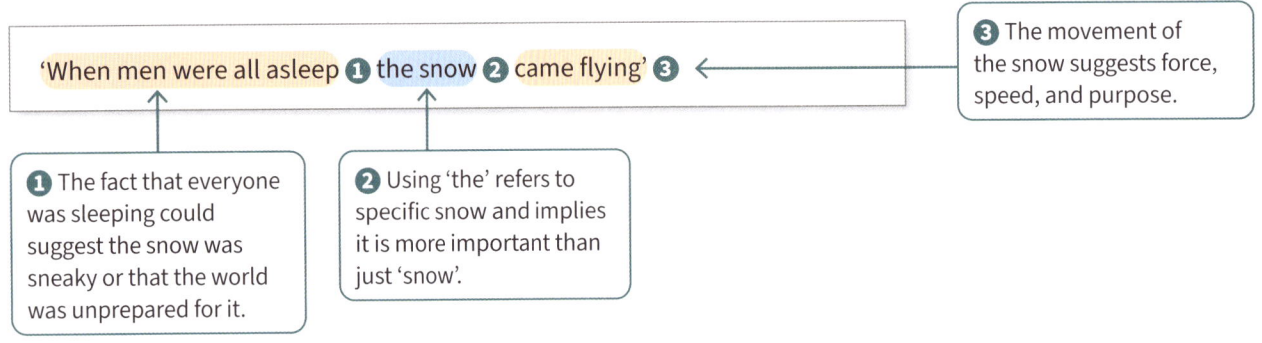

'When men were all asleep ❶ the snow ❷ came flying' ❸

❶ The fact that everyone was sleeping could suggest the snow was sneaky or that the world was unprepared for it.

❷ Using 'the' refers to specific snow and implies it is more important than just 'snow'.

❸ The movement of the snow suggests force, speed, and purpose.

Connotation

A **connotation** is an idea or a feeling that is often connected to, or associated with, a word or phrase, in addition to its main explicit meaning. This is shown in the poem 'London Snow'.

'When men were all asleep the snow came flying'

The idea of being asleep while snow is falling has connotations of Christmas, surprise gifts, and childhood. Its use here creates a feeling of excitement and magic.

Analysing repetition

A poet may choose to repeat a sound, word, or phrase within the same line of a poem or at particular points within the whole poem. How the poet positions them can help create rhythm, for example, if they are placed at the start or end of each stanza, or as standalone lines.

'The eye marvelled—marvelled at the dazzling whiteness'

In this line from 'London Snow', the repetition of 'marvelled' emphasises what a special and wonderful sight the speaker feels the snow creates.

Alliteration

Alliteration is the repetition of the same consonant or sound at the beginning of a group of words. This example is from 'London Snow'.

'Silently sifting and veiling road, roof and railing'

Two examples of alliteration are used: the repetition of 's' conveys ideas of the snow's gentle, quiet movement. The repetition of 'r' creates a rolling sound to describe the things the snow covers. These create an idea for the reader of the motion of the events within the poem.

Assonance

Assonance is the repetition of similar vowel sounds across neighbouring words. It can be in any part of the words. This example is from 'London Snow'.

'Silently sifting and veiling road, roof and railing'

The assonance in this line is found through the 'ai' sound using 'ei' and 'ai'. It adds to the lyrical feeling in the poem and builds rhyme within lines as well as across the ends of them.

Key terms — Make sure you can write a definition for these key terms

analyse   connotation   explicit   implicit   inferred

Knowledge CONCEPT

5 Language

Consonance

Consonance is the repetition of similar consonant sounds across neighbouring words. It can be in any part of the words.

> 'Stealthily and perpetually settling and loosely lying'

The consonance in this line from 'London Snow' is found at both the end and start of some of the words in the repetition of 'ly'. The effect is to slow down the rhythm of the line and focus the reader more closely on the image being created.

Anaphora

Anaphora is a particular type of repetition where a word or phrase is used in phrases, clauses, or sentences that follow one another immediately.

> 'Their minds diverted; the daily word is unspoken,
> The daily thoughts of labour and sorrow slumber'

Robert Bridges repeats the sentence format, as well as 'daily', but changes from 'word' to 'thoughts'. This creates the idea that the snow has changed everything in the men's daily routine and given them a brief gift that has made them forget to both talk about and even think about their worries.

LINK
Refresh your memory about anaphora as a structural device on page 22.

Rhyme

Rhyme is created through the repetition of sounds in words. It is often used at the end of lines and, depending on which lines rhyme, creates the rhyme scheme of the poem. The rhyme scheme created below is ABAB – alternate lines rhyme.

> 'When men were all asleep the snow came flying, ❶
> In large white flakes falling on the city brown, ❷
> Stealthily and perpetually settling and loosely lying, ❶
> Hushing the latest traffic of the drowsy town' ❷

❶ The long 'i' sound is repeated in the verbs that end lines 1 and 3, as well as the '-ing' sound.

❷ The 'ow' sound is repeated in the nouns and adjectives ending lines 2 and 4.

In these lines from 'London Snow', the verbs make the snow sound active and the nouns make the town sound passive: using rhyme draws attention to these words, so the effect of the rhyme is to emphasise these qualities.

LINK
Refresh your memory of rhyme and rhythm on pages 20–21.

Onomatopoeia

Onomatopoeia means words that imitate the sound of what they stand for. Onomatopoeia often contributes to sensory meaning within a poem and helps create vivid images. The following examples are from 'London Snow'.

'Hushing the latest traffic of the drowsy town'

The use of 'hushing' suggests the snow has a gentle, quieting effect on the world.

'With lessened load a few carts creak and blunder,'

The use of 'creak' allows the poet to convey the noise of the cartwheels to conjure an audible image for the reader, without a long, detailed description.

Sibilance

Sibilance is when a hissing sound is created through the repetition of letters such as 's', 'sh', 'ch', or 'z'. It can contribute to the mood and rhythm of a poem by emphasising particular syllables, and directing how the poem should be read. Sibilance is used in 'London Snow'.

'Silently sifting'

The repeated use of 's' here is both alliterative and sibilant. It creates a gentle and rhythmic quality to mimic the falling snow.

'Lazily and incessantly floating down and down'

The combined use of 'ces' and 's' has a particular impact on the word 'incessantly'. Two instances of the 's' sound draw out the word and emphasise its literal meaning of 'continuing without interruption' – the word feels drawn out and unstoppable.

> **REVISION TIP**
>
> When analysing the methods in a poem, make sure you link those methods to why the writer uses them, and how they create meaning and effect.

Refrain

Refrain is when a whole line is repeated within a poem. This is often at the end of stanzas, but can be at any point in the poem, or at regular intervals. This example is from 'The Highwayman'.

And the highwayman came riding—

                Riding—riding—

These lines are repeated three times and contribute to the rhythm of the poem. As they occur near the start, middle, and end of the poem, they also keep an active image of the highwayman himself in the reader's mind.

Key terms — Make sure you can write a definition for these key terms:

alliteration   assonance   consonance   onomatopoeia   refrain   sibilance

Knowledge CONCEPT

5 Language

Analysing comparative language

Poets use particular comparative language techniques to create **imagery** in their poems. Other language techniques then support and enhance these images. Comparison can take many forms: just as meaning can be read in 'layers', comparisons often have layers to peel away. By doing this, the bigger meaning of the poem can be revealed.

Simile

A **simile** creates an image by directly comparing one thing to another. Similes always do this using 'like', 'as', 'as if', or 'than'.

> 'His eyes were hollows of madness, his hair like mouldy hay'

In 'The Highwayman', this unpleasant comparison is made of the man's hair to decaying, dried grass. This helps the reader imagine that his hair shares the same qualities as the hay: smelly, damp, and dull in colour. However, it also suggests something about his character: that the man is unattractive and unlikeable.

Metaphor

A **metaphor** is a comparison of two things which creates an image without using comparative words. Instead, a metaphor will say one thing actually *is* something else.

> 'The road was a ribbon of moonlight'

There are two elements in this metaphor to describe the road in 'The Highwayman': 'moonlight' allows the reader to imagine that the road stands out clearly in the dark night and is lit by the moon, or is white like moonlight; 'ribbon' describes the way the road moves across the landscape, curling and curving.

REVISION TIP

Extended metaphors can be developed across a whole poem. During your revision, practise scanning poems for vocabulary that could be connected. It may be evidence of an extended metaphor.

Extended metaphor

An extended metaphor can be created by placing several images which connect to the same idea across a poem, or by building up a metaphor by giving more description.

'The moon was a ghostly galleon ❶ tossed upon cloudy seas.' ❷

❶ This metaphor from 'The Highwayman' is used to compare the moon to a ghost ship, suggesting it is glowing white in the sky and building an eerie and gothic atmosphere.

❷ It becomes an extended metaphor because additional detail is given to build up the comparative image being created: 'cloudy seas' could suggest it is a cloudy night, and clouds are passing across the moon; 'tossed' describes the movement of the clouds, suggesting it is a windy night and the moon looks like it is being buffeted, just like waves would break against a ship on the sea and rock it.

Oxymoron

An **oxymoron** is a phrase created by pairing two directly contrasting words, such as 'bitter-sweet' or 'random order'. The opposing meanings create striking and sometimes humorous images, and make the reader think more deeply about the meaning.

'Hiding difference, making unevenness even'

These words from 'London Snow' are direct opposites. By combining them, the reader is challenged to imagine how the snow falling is slowly erasing the difference in height between objects.

Antithesis

Antithesis is created when two directly contrasting ideas are placed closely together for comparison. The opposing meanings create striking images and make the reader think more deeply about the meaning.

'The ear hearkened to the stillness of the solemn air'

To 'hearken' is to 'listen carefully', but the sound which is being listened to in 'London Snow' is the absence of sound in the air – 'the stillness'. This draws attention to the fact that, as snow absorbs sound, nothing can be heard. This is a rare thing in a city and is therefore special.

Key terms Make sure you can write a definition for these key terms

antithesis imagery metaphor
oxymoron simile

Knowledge CONCEPT

5 Language

Analysing figurative language

Imagery can also use figurative language techniques that allow the poet to represent ideas, emotions, and meanings in creative ways. These techniques can bring objects to life and give them a purpose that is beyond their everyday meaning. They allow a poet to **exaggerate**, build depth and atmosphere, and create emotional or comic moments.

Personification

Personification is when a non-human object or abstract idea is described as though it has human qualities.

> 'the sun, in pale display
> Standing by Paul's high dome, spread forth below
> His sparkling beams, and awoke the stir of the day.'

The sun is personified in 'London Snow', as its light appears across the scene. It is described as though it is acting deliberately by shining on the snow and waking the world.

Pathetic fallacy

Pathetic fallacy is when human feelings are given to objects, things in nature, or animals.

> 'the sun admitted,
> I am just a shadow.
> I wish I could show you'

In 'My Brilliant Image', the words 'admitted' and 'I am' suggest the sun can think and talk, while 'I wish' shows it has desire and emotion.

Hyperbole

Hyperbole is language that exaggerates a situation to add emphasis or to create a humorous image.

> 'They […] rioted in a drift, plunging up to the knees'

In 'London Snow', the behaviour of schoolboys playing in the snow is described using hyperbole to exaggerate their excitement and enthusiastic behaviour in enjoying the sudden snow. A literal riot is a violent public disturbance: 'rioted' therefore suggests unrestrained fun, where the snow is thrown, jumped in, and generally disturbed.

Symbolism

Symbolism is created in poetry when an emotion or idea is represented through a symbol. A symbol can be many different things, such as an object, a person, a colour, or something from the natural world.

'Plaiting a dark ❶ red ❷ love-knot into her long black hair.'

'A red-coat ❷ troop came marching'

'Blood red ❷ were his spurs in the golden noon; wine-red ❷ was his velvet coat'

❶ Darkness is used throughout 'The Highwayman' as a symbol or warning of doom and death.

❷ The poet repeats the colour red throughout the poem. Red is used to symbolise both the passionate love between the highwayman and Bess, but it also symbolises death. The redcoats shoot the highwayman and cause Bess's death.

'The road ❶ was a ribbon of moonlight ❷ […] When the road ❶ was a gypsy's ribbon […] For the road ❶ lay bare ❷ in the moonlight' ❷

❶ The road itself symbolises freedom, rebellion, danger, and violence, as it is the place where the highwayman robs travellers, but also meets his death.

❷ The road is often described in ways that make it stand out as white or moonlit. This provides a contrast with other symbolic colours in the poem, such as red, and helps each symbol stand out. This shows how poets might combine techniques to create stronger or more meaningful effect.

Irony

Irony is when the poem's true meaning is the opposite of the words actually used. Readers must look for the implied meaning, using the rest of the poem as context to help understand what that meaning is. For example, 'Ozymandias' by Percy Bysshe Shelley, is a poem about a great ruler described as 'King of Kings', yet ironically, his statue lies ruined and forgotten in a desert.

Dramatic irony can be created in poems when the reader has a greater awareness of events than the character(s) within the poem.

'I'll come to thee by moonlight, though hell should bar the way.'

The highwayman **foreshadows** the trouble that will lie ahead when he returns to Bess, which creates dramatic irony for the reader, who knows when the soldiers arrive and imprison Bess, they are the 'hell' that will stop the highwayman from getting to her.

Key terms	Make sure you can write a definition for these key terms	dramatic irony exaggerate foreshadow hyperbole irony pathetic fallacy personification

Knowledge CONCEPT

5 Language

Analysing word choice

The poet will have made a conscious choice in every word they use in their poem. Sometimes words are functional and mean only what a reader might expect, but often they are full of implicit meaning and feeling. It is important to think about the meanings and feelings created by individual words, and by combinations of words across a line, stanza, or even the whole poem.

Sensory language

Sensory language is words and phrases that appeal to the five core human senses: touch, taste, smell, hearing, sight.

Two other senses are connected to the sense of touch: motion and balance, and body awareness. These may also be explored in images that relate to how something moves or its place in connection to things around it.

Sensory language is an essential part of building strong imagery because it creates a close, physical connection between the reader and the ideas of the poem.

Touch

> 'A coat of the claret velvet, and breeches of brown doe-skin.'

The highwayman's clothes are described using the materials they are made from, to convey that they are pleasing to the touch, hint at their expense and quality, and imply he's a successful robber. Touch is often used to give a sense of what lies beneath a surface or to show how a character is experiencing the world or another character.

Taste

> 'They gathered up the crystal manna to freeze
> Their tongues with tasting'

In 'London Snow' the poet chooses 'manna' to describe the snow the boys eat. This implies that the snow is like a miracle sent from heaven.

Taste can often be symbolic of something else as well as intensifying the reader's experience. Here, it is also combined with the sense of touch: 'freeze'.

Smell

> 'As the black cascade of perfume came tumbling over his breast'

In 'The Highwayman', Bess's long hair is the black cascade that falls over the highwayman as she leans down to kiss him. The reference to perfume shows this was a sensory experience for the highwayman and deepens the image that they share a passionate, intoxicating love. Smell is often used in relation to the natural world, or to suggest animal or instinctive behaviour.

Hearing

'Tlot-tlot; tlot-tlot! ❶ Had they heard it? The horsehoofs ringing clear' ❷

❶ Onomatopoeia is often used in imagery because it helps convey the sound exactly as the ear would hear it. In 'The Highwayman', it also dramatises events in telling the reader what is happening: the highwayman, whom the soldiers are waiting for, is riding into the trap.

❷ Describing the hoofs

LINK

Refresh your memory of onomatopoeia on page 27.

Sight

'And all woke earlier for the unaccustomed brightness
Of the winter dawning, the strange unheavenly glare'

Poets make word choices to describe what is seen in order to develop an idea, intensify an image, or say something about the viewer, such as how their emotions, hopes, or judgements affect the way they see things.
In 'London Snow', the poet shows how the snow has affected the experience of sunrise. A winter dawning would usually be weak light; the snow is so bright it creates light that is as bright as heaven, yet is 'unheavenly' because it is created on Earth.

Motion and balance

'And the highwayman came riding—
    Riding—riding—'

Motion intensifies the reader's experience and a poet may use it to build a sense of realistic movement, or to convey the physical experience of a character. It can also contribute to the mood of the poem.
Repetition is used in 'The Highwayman' to recreate the rhythm of the highwayman's galloping movement on his horse. It helps the reader visualise his motion in the poem, creating a more realistic character and scene. It also creates rhythm when reading the poem itself.

Body awareness

'Over the cobbles he clattered and clashed in the dark inn-yard.'

The position of the highwayman in the scene is connected to him riding a horse. By focusing on the 'cobbles', the reader will zoom in on the horse's hooves, then 'in the dark inn-yard', zoom out so the reader can see the man and horse fully in context.

The positioning of important elements in a poem helps bring the story to life and, in this example, gives it the quality of a film that tells a story.

Knowledge CONCEPT

5 Language

Emotive vocabulary

Emotive vocabulary is the words that are chosen for their emotional effect on the reader. Often a poet wants to share a particular message with the reader and wants them to respond in a particular way. They will therefore use words that should direct and control how the reader feels, for example, to make them feel joyful, scared, excited, angered, in awe, or repulsed.

> 'She **twisted** her hands behind her; but all the knots held good!
> She **writhed** her hands till her fingers were wet with sweat or blood!
> They **stretched** and **strained** in the darkness'

These verbs from 'The Highwayman' show a squirming, frantic effort to convey Bess's emotional desperation. The poet wants the reader to share Bess's urgent fear that she must escape, so that when Bess finally reaches for the trigger of the gun, the reader understands why Bess might make the decision to shoot herself.

Wordplay

Wordplay is when words are manipulated and used for comic effect. There are different types of wordplay, including:

- malapropism – when a similar-sounding word is used to replace the intended word for comic effect, such as 'Dynamite is a girl's best friend', rather than 'Diamonds'.
- double entendre – when words with more than one meaning are used ambiguously, so the true meaning is unclear and a sexual inference can be made.
- puns – when the different meanings of a word, or words that sound the same, are used to clever and humorous effect.

> 'They had tied her up **to attention**'

In 'The Highwayman', the soldiers trying to kill the highwayman tie up Bess so she stands vertically 'to attention'. This plays on the idea that soldiers often stand to attention while waiting. This has a darkly humorous effect, but also creates pathos.

Nouns

> 'men […] city […] **snow** […] lightness'

Some nouns are chosen for their necessity: 'snow' in 'London Snow' is only snow, for example.

> '**cobbles** […] whip […] Bess […] dog'

In 'The Highwayman', the poet chose 'cobbles' (instead of, for example, 'ground' or 'floor') to create a rhythm through alliteration in the line 'Over the cobbles he clattered and clashed'. Therefore, the noun choice has a creative impact in helping the reader to imagine the texture of the inn-yard floor and the sound of the hooves.

Verbs

'flying […] blew off […] freeze'

Verbs help a poem become a physical thing because they introduce the action and movement within it. The reader unconsciously responds to verbs, so if they are gentle then the reader feels more relaxed and moves along with the rhythm of the poem. If they are aggressive or sudden, then the reader feels more on edge and may read the poem with more anticipation or anxiety about what will happen. This is intensified with the addition of adverbs.

Adverbs

'Stealthily and perpetually settling and loosely lying'

'Yet, if they press me sharply'

These adverbs in 'London Snow' give more detail on how the snow settles and forms on the ground. The effect of using adverbs is to build a more vivid and precise picture than the verbs alone would give.

This adverb in 'The Highwayman' suggests that the soldiers will pursue the highwayman aggressively, and it creates a physical sensation in the image being created. This also mirrors the sharpness of the soldiers' swords.

> **REVISION TIP**
> When analysing poems, don't look for word classes: look for interesting vocabulary choices that connect to the question focus. Only then consider whether there is a link to the word class and whether the poet has used it as a particular tool.

Adjectives

'In large white flakes falling on the city brown'

'He'd a French cocked-hat on his forehead, a bunch of lace at his chin,
A coat of the claret velvet, and breeches of brown doe-skin.'

Colour adjectives in 'London Snow' create a visual and emotional contrast between the dull city and the pure brightness of the snow. They help build the mood that something special is taking place.

Adjectives in 'The Highwayman' build a richer image of the highwayman and his stylish manner of dress. This has a visual effect for the reader and strengthens his position as a central character.

5 Knowledge 35

Knowledge

CONCEPT

5 Language

Punctuation and capitalisation

- Poets may use punctuation formally, beginning lines with capital letters and ending with full stops.
- Poets may not use any punctuation or capital letters at all.
- Particular words might be capitalised to show their importance or to encourage emphasis.
- Commas help the flow of the poem, creating natural pauses to breathe, but also separating ideas.
- Brackets might have the effect of an 'aside' to the reader or share the poet's thoughts.
- An ellipsis may create a pause for reflection or to create suspense.
- Semi-colons allow briefer pauses and may encourage the reader to consider the following words more closely.
- Colons are more demanding and can direct the reader's attention more forcefully to the words that follow.
- Quotation marks may show speech, or may be used around words to suggest irony, or show the speaker is challenging the idea.
- Single or paired dashes can allow asides, give extra details, create interruptions, or increase the informality of a poem.

REMEMBER
Only write about punctuation and capitalisation if you can explore how these contribute towards meaning and if it is relevant to the question you are answering.

Key terms Make sure you can write a definition for these key term

sensory

Retrieval

5

Answer the questions below. Cover the answers column with a piece of paper and write down as many answers as you can. Check and repeat.

Questions | Answers

#	Question	Answer
1	What is the difference between literal meaning and implicit meaning in poetry?	Literal meaning is obvious and stated clearly by the words or phrases; implicit meaning might be implied, suggested, or hinted at by the poet
2	What is a connotation?	An idea or a feeling that is often connected to or associated with a word or phrase, in addition to its main explicit meaning
3	What technique is being used in this example? He put his feet on my seat.	Assonance – the long 'e' vowel sound is repeated in 'feet' and 'seat'
4	What is created through the repetition of sounds in words?	Rhyme
5	Why might a poet choose to use onomatopoeia?	To contribute to sensory meaning within a poem and help create vivid images
6	How does simile create comparison?	It helps the reader imagine that the things being compared share the same qualities
7	What effect do figurative language techniques such as personification have when creating imagery?	They can bring objects to life and give them a purpose that is beyond their everyday meaning
8	What is symbolism?	When an emotion or idea is represented through a symbol, such as an object, a person, a colour, or something from the natural world
9	What kind of meaning is present in irony?	Implied meaning
10	Explain why sensory language is an important part of building strong imagery	Because it creates a close, physical connection between the reader and the ideas of the poem

Previous questions

Now go back and use these questions to check your knowledge of previous topics.

Questions | Answers

#	Question	Answer
1	What is enjambment?	When there is no punctuation at the end of a line and the sentence or phrase continues into the next line
2	What is an end-stopped line?	A line that ends with a piece of punctuation or is a complete phrase

Knowledge — EXAM

6 Exam overview

Key exam paper information

In the exam, there will be one question on one unseen poem and one question comparing this poem with a second unseen poem. You must answer *both* questions.

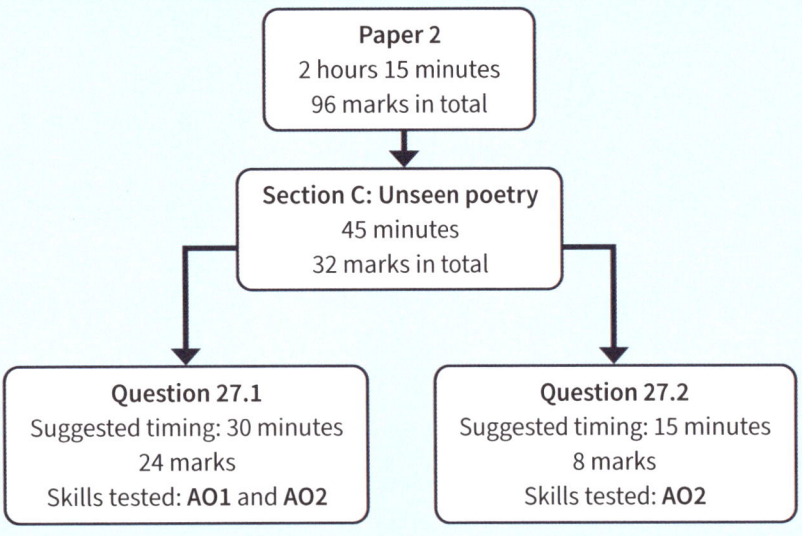

EXAM TIP

You can spend about 30 minutes on Question 27.1 – but this should include time for reading the poem and planning. Consider allowing 10 minutes to read and plan, and 20 minutes for writing your response.

Assessment objectives

Exam questions are carefully constructed to allow you to demonstrate your skills. Behind each question is a set of assessment objectives.

Assessment objective	Explanation	What this means in the unseen poetry section of the exam
AO1	How well you answer the question and understand the text	• You will show how well you understand the poem and the poet's ideas, and will write about them in relation to the task.
AO1	How well you choose parts of the text to support your answer	• You will give examples from the poem to back up your points. This can be summaries, paraphrases, or direct quotations. They should be kept short.
AO2	How well you explain what each poet has done to create meanings	• You will explore the methods used by each poet, and how they have them to create meaning in their poems.
AO2	Your use of subject vocabulary linked to meanings	• You will use words like poem, lines, words, and stanzas to show that you are writing about a poem. • You can also use more complex vocabulary if you wish to, but this is not needed for high marks.

Questions

These are examples of the two question types. They relate to the poems on pages 42–43 and 56.

Q27.1 Respond to a poem and comment on how meaning is created

This question relates to poem 1 and tests both AO1 and AO2.

> In 'Poem at Thirty-nine', how does the poet present the speaker's feelings about her father?
>
> [24 marks]

EXAM TIP

It is really important that you don't just write about the poem – you must analyse it using the question focus.

This question tests your ability to:
- understand a poem and the ideas, messages, and meanings within it
- write critically to analyse a poem against a task
- recognise the methods a poet uses to craft a poem
- comment on a wide range of language, form, and structural techniques
- understand the effects of the poet's methods
- use relevant subject terminology to help support your explanation and analysis
- support your analysis using references to the text.

Q27.2 Compare the methods used in two poems to create meaning and effect

This question relates to poem 1 and poem 2; it tests AO2.

> In both 'Poem at Thirty-nine' and 'Those Winter Sundays', the speakers describe their feelings about appreciating their fathers.
>
> What are the similarities and/or differences between the methods the poets use to present these feelings?
>
> [8 marks]

REVISION TIP

You should spend about 30 minutes on Question 27.1 and 15 minutes on Question 27.2, but you can adjust this to suit you. Time yourself during your revision, so you know how long you want to allocate to each question in the exam.

This question tests your ability to:
- recognise the methods a poet uses to craft a poem
- understand the effects of the poet's methods
- compare and contrast methods used across two different poems to present a particular idea, feeling, or attitude
- use relevant subject terminology to help support your explanation and analysis
- support your analysis using references to the text.

LINK

Refresh your memory with the concept section on pages 8–37, which will remind you of the different methods a poet may use in their writing, including language, form, and structural techniques.

Knowledge EXAM

7 Analysing one poem

Strategies

When you analyse the first poem, you need to peel away the layers. There are many strategies to choose from to help you do this.

Here are some strategies you could use.

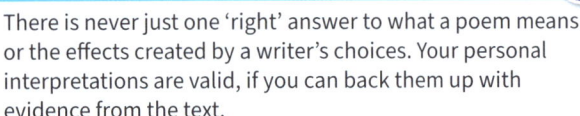

- Read the poem several times, annotating it with things that jump out on each reading.
- Focus on how the poet presents ideas, feelings, attitudes, or effects on the particular topic or thematic area identified in the question.
- Analyse the poem in one slower reading, stanza by stanza.
- Create boxes or bullet lists to categorise things you notice as you read, such as: your reactions as a reader; the poet's message, lesson, or attitude; important language methods; important structural methods.

EXAM TIP

In the exam, use the strategy that works best for you and that you are most familiar with – this will help you feel more confident.

REMEMBER

In the exam, remember that you should:
- read the question
- analyse the text
- plan your answer
- write your response
- check your response.

REVISION TIP

There is never just one 'right' answer to what a poem means or the effects created by a writer's choices. Your personal interpretations are valid, if you can back them up with evidence from the text.

Example step-by-step analysis

As you have seen, there are a huge number of poetic elements and methods to potentially comment on.

Question 27.1 asks you to focus on how the poet uses some of these elements and methods to present ideas, feelings, attitudes, or effects on a particular topic or thematic area.

You need to be aware of the many different ways a poet can work, but be selective in your analysis.

Here is an example of how a strategy using three read-throughs of the poem might build up analysis of the poem. For each read-through, there are examples of the types of questions you might ask yourself. You would not try to answer all of these questions in an exam situation, but they will help you to refine your analysis skills during revision, and show how you can build up ideas.

EXAM TIP

Keep the question focus clearly in mind. Don't waste time analysing every line of the poem in detail: if it doesn't relate to the topic of the question, don't include it in your answer.

First read-through

Respond: What are your first impressions?

GOAL: To understand the poem at a literal level

- Who is speaking?
- Who are they speaking to?
- Does the title give you any information?
- What's the poem about?
- Does it have an obvious purpose, such as telling a story or recounting a memory?
- Gut reaction – how does the poem make you feel?

> **REVISION TIP**
>
> Write down easy-to-remember key steps for your preferred analysis strategy, for example:
> - Respond: Who? What? Why?
> - Analyse: Voice, form, words, patterns, images
> - Evaluate: Message, tone, atmosphere

Second read-through

Evaluate: What does it mean?

GOAL: To bring together ideas about meaning and reader response

- What is the poet's main message?
- What is the poet's attitude, tone, and purpose?
- What atmosphere is created in the poem – and does it change?
- What mood does the poem create in you?

Third read-through

Analyse: What stands out?

GOAL: To identify elements that might have meaning and to think about how the poem has been constructed

- How does the poem sit on the page? Short or long stanzas? Differing line lengths? Lines end-stopped or enjambed? Unusual layout? Lots of space? No space?
- Are there any lines that clearly show the idea, feeling, or attitude the question is asking about?
- Is the poem a recognisable form or genre?
- Is there anything you don't understand?
- What tense and voice (first/second/third person) are used?
- What's the tone of the voice?
- What images are being created that show something about the question focus?
- Is there any allusion or contextual references?
- What words or phrases stand out to you, and why?
- Is there a noticeable rhythm or rhyme scheme?
- Are there any other patterns?
- Are there any obvious contrasts?
- How does the poem start and how does it end? Do they connect?

> **REVISION TIP**
>
> Try to 'hear' the poem by reading it aloud in your head. Sometimes it can help to imagine someone reading it whose voice you know well. This will help you to recognise the rhythm and rhyme of the poem, and any words that are given particular emphasis.

Knowledge EXAM

7 Analysing one poem

Sample analysis of poem 1

Below is a sample question and poem. A student has analysed the question and poem using some of the analysis questions on page 41.

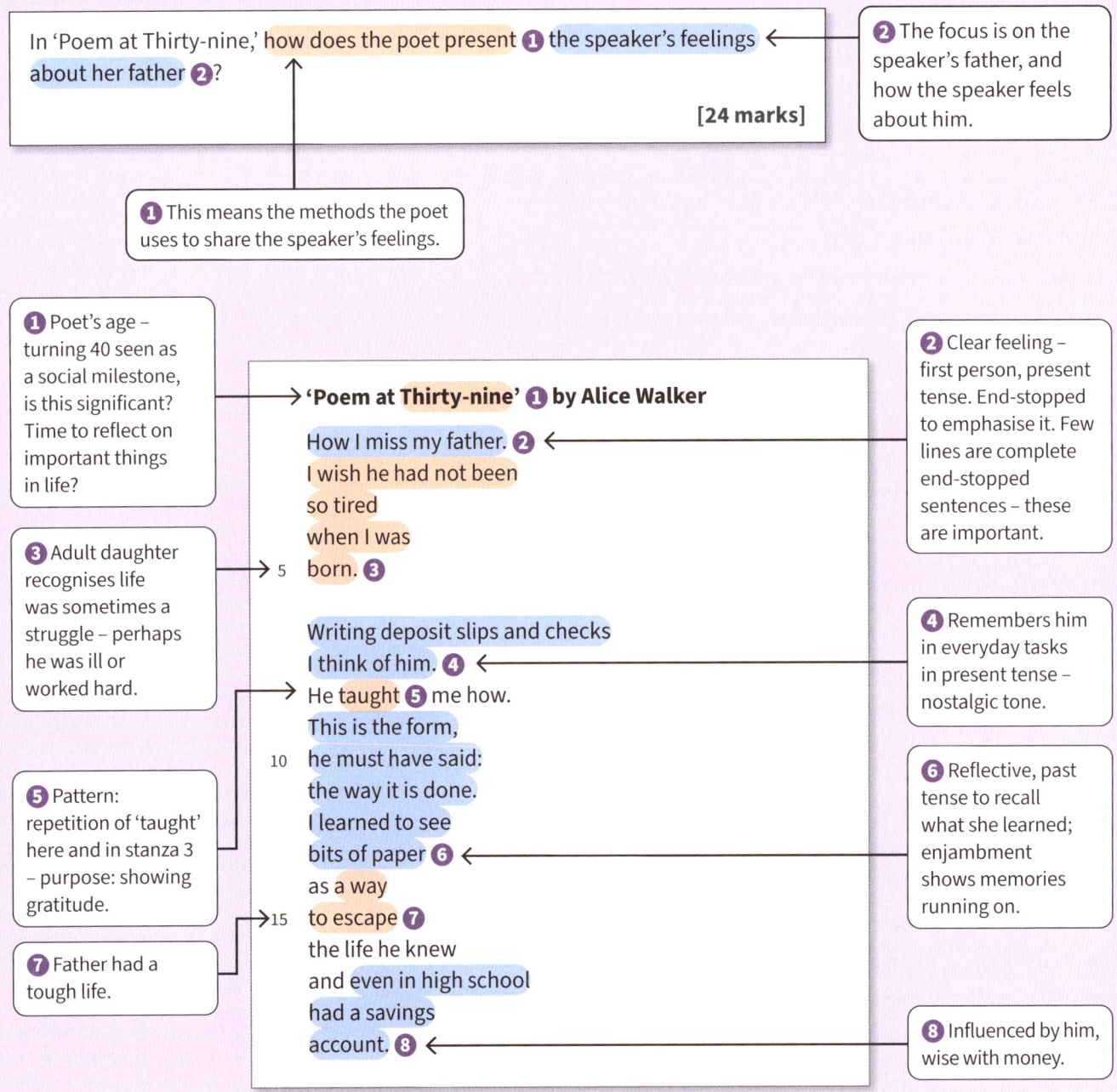

In 'Poem at Thirty-nine,' how does the poet present ❶ the speaker's feelings about her father ❷?

[24 marks]

❷ The focus is on the speaker's father, and how the speaker feels about him.

❶ This means the methods the poet uses to share the speaker's feelings.

❶ Poet's age – turning 40 seen as a social milestone, is this significant? Time to reflect on important things in life?

❸ Adult daughter recognises life was sometimes a struggle – perhaps he was ill or worked hard.

❺ Pattern: repetition of 'taught' here and in stanza 3 – purpose: showing gratitude.

❼ Father had a tough life.

'Poem at Thirty-nine' ❶ by Alice Walker

How I miss my father. ❷
I wish he had not been
so tired
when I was
5 born. ❸

Writing deposit slips and checks
I think of him. ❹
He taught ❺ me how.
This is the form,
10 he must have said:
the way it is done.
I learned to see
bits of paper ❻
as a way
15 to escape ❼
the life he knew
and even in high school
had a savings
account. ❽

❷ Clear feeling – first person, present tense. End-stopped to emphasise it. Few lines are complete end-stopped sentences – these are important.

❹ Remembers him in everyday tasks in present tense – nostalgic tone.

❻ Reflective, past tense to recall what she learned; enjambment shows memories running on.

❽ Influenced by him, wise with money.

9 Does 'always' suggest he did sometimes beat her for telling the truth? Seems to be highlighting that he valued truth and was a good man.

11 Simile creates a vibrant and slightly crazy image: calm but joyful; she's celebrating him – poem now changes, second half is light-hearted.

14 Extended metaphor of cooking represents her approach to life – she takes his literal cooking and uses it to make her life better, and to pass it on. Rhyme/half rhymes created within these lines give a distinctive rhythm.

20 He taught me
    that telling the truth
    did not always mean
    a beating; **9**
    though many of my truths
25 must have grieved him
    before the end.

    How I miss my father! **10**
    He cooked like a person
    dancing
30 in a yoga meditation **11**
    and craved the voluptuous **12**
    sharing
    of good food. **13**

    Now I look and cook just like him:
35 my brain light;
    tossing this and that
    into the pot;
    seasoning none of my life
    the same way twice; happy to feed
40 whoever strays my way. **14**

    He would have grown
    to admire **15**
    the woman I've become:
    cooking, writing, chopping wood,
45 staring into the fire.

10 Pattern: repetition of phrase, exclamation mark emphasises she really misses him.

12 Adjective – very few in poem. Their relationship created through action.

13 He was a generous man, as shown in vocabulary choices.

15 Feels he would have been proud, regrets he isn't here to see her.

EXAM TIP

You could use different-coloured highlighters or underlining to help separate out different areas such as language or structural choices.

7 Knowledge

Knowledge

7 Analysing one poem

How to write about one unseen poem

Once you have annotated a poem with your ideas, you need to choose the best ideas to write up in your response. Always read the exam question again before you make this choice: it will help keep you focused on what your points should be about.

Remember there should be four parts to each point you make when answering Question 27.1:

- the idea, feeling, or attitude that is shown in the poem
- the method or technique the poet has used to show it
- the effect of the method or technique
- textual references from the poem.

In your answer, it can help to lead with the idea, feeling, or attitude, then to talk about the technique. If you start with the technique, it's easier to lose focus on the point you are trying to make.

> **REVISION TIP**
>
> Practise planning as part of your revision and develop a technique that works for you. The more you practise, the easier and faster you will find it to plan, which will be a real benefit in the exam.

> **REVISION TIP**
>
> Look back over previous answers you have written – this could include your Anthology poetry. Look at your points critically: if you spot any points where you lead with the technique but lose focus, try rewriting them and making the idea, feeling, or attitude come first. Does it help the clarity of your response?

On pages 45–49 are examples of how some of the annotations on 'Poem at Thirty-nine' on pages 42–43 could be written up into points in an exam answer. On the left is a lower-level response, and on the right is a higher-level response. The examiner's comments explain the strengths of each response and how improvements could be made.

> In 'Poem at Thirty-nine', how does the poet present the speaker's feelings about her father?
>
> **[24 marks]**

Example 1

Feeling shown towards father: Nostalgic affection and gratitude

Method/technique: Structural – free verse

> **LINK**
> Refresh your memory of free verse and enjambment on pages 18 and 22.

Lower-level point	Example in poem	Higher-level point
Free verse is used by the poet so she can say anything without having to make it rhyme, when she's just having thoughts rather than planning it all out.	Whole poem written in free verse	The poet captures a strong feeling of nostalgia towards the speaker's father by presenting her poem in free verse. This form allows her memories to spill out freely and without any restriction, reflecting her feelings of gratitude and affection towards her father which similarly spill out throughout the poem.
Examiner's comments: The student recognises a technique that has been used and explains its effects in a basic way. However, they aren't commenting at all on a feeling that is created.		**Examiner's comments:** Beginning with the feeling helps the student to focus on the question requirement. They make a clear connection between how free verse works and how human thoughts and the memory process work, using the idea of 'spilling out'.

Method/technique: Structural – enjambment

Lower-level point	Example in poem	Higher-level point
Enjambment is really important in this poem because the poet uses enjambment most of the time to make the lines run on like it's her thinking.	Only three lines are end-stopped, rest are enjambed	The speaker's pleasant memories about her father are enhanced through frequent enjambment, which allows her memories to cross the lines. This has the effect that she is remembering as she is writing – there's an occasional hesitancy 'this is the form / he must have said'. This makes the feelings seem more real and draws the reader in to experience the memory together with the speaker.
Examiner's comments: Correct terminology used and understanding of its deliberate use across the poem. However, more needs to be said to explain 'like it's her thinking' to show what feeling is being explored and exactly how enjambment contributes to this feeling.		**Examiner's comments:** This answer is strong because it is analysing both how the poet has used enjambment structurally and how it shows what the speaker is doing and feeling within the poem. The student shows real insight into the poet's approach and uses a relevant quotation to describe the effect on the reader.

Knowledge — EXAM

7 Analysing one poem

Example 2

Feeling shown towards father: She misses him and he had an important effect on her.

Method/technique: Perspective – use of first person

> **LINK**
> Refresh your memory of first person, present tense, and past tense on pages 14–15.

Lower-level point	Example in poem	Higher-level point
We know she feels sad because she says 'I miss my father'. This is in the first person so we know it's how she feels.	'How I miss my father.'	We know the speaker is feeling sad that her father is not around because she states it directly at the beginning of the poem: 'How I miss my father'. The present tense makes her emotion feel very real and fresh and the word 'how' deepens the impression that she still feels very strongly about her father.
Examiner's comments: The student understands the feeling shown and the basic effect of present tense, but needs to think about these things more deeply. They should consider the effect of the perspective and could also consider how this idea is repeated elsewhere in the poem and the effect of that.		**Examiner's comments:** The student explains the effect of the chosen perspective clearly. They carefully consider the quotation to show the meaning the reader can take from this one line in the poem.

Method/technique: Perspective – use of present tense and past tense

Lower-level point	Example in poem	Higher-level point
When she's showing different feelings like remembering good things her dad did and then what she does when she's cooking now, the poet sometimes uses present tense and sometimes uses past tense. This is so we know the difference between memories and what is happening now to her.	'he taught me' 'Now I look and cook just like him'	The poet recollects many moments she shared with her father in the past where 'he taught me', but then contrasts these with where she is in the present and what she is like. Moving between the past and present tense allows her to reflect on the effect of time, and how she has grown as a result of her father's nurture and influence so that she is someone he'd be proud of: 'Now I look and cook just like him'.
Examiner's comments: The student has tried to explore how the poet uses past and present tense to move between memories and the present day, but they haven't added the explanation and evaluation that is needed. Some well-chosen quotations might help the student focus on what they mean, and give them something concrete to analyse.		**Examiner's comments:** Present and past tense can be simply functional, but in this poem, the poet uses them for a particular purpose. This is important – only comment on techniques that have purpose in the poem you are exploring AND relate to the question focus. Here, the student has identified how changing perspective creates contrast and builds a particular impression within the poem.

Example 3

Feeling towards father: Her father taught her important things.

Method/technique: Repetition of words 'taught' and 'learned'

> **LINK**
> Refresh your memory of repetition on pages 25–27.

Lower-level point	Example in poem	Higher-level point
The poet repeats the word 'taught' and also uses the word 'learned'. This shows me he was a good dad who wanted her to know things.	'He taught me how.' 'I learned to see / bits of paper / as a way / to escape' 'He taught me that telling the truth did not always mean a beating'	The speaker states directly that she feels she learned important things from her father by repeating the words 'taught' and 'learned'. These things include practical skills such as filling in forms – 'He taught me how' – but also valuable moral lessons, when she reveals 'He taught me that telling the truth did not always mean a beating'. This final image is slightly unsettling. It could be interpreted that there were times telling the truth did result in the speaker being hit, or it could suggest that her father had been beaten for telling the truth and therefore did not parent her in the same way. This would link to the speaker's feeling that her father had a tough life and she 'learned to see' that he had had to 'escape the life he knew'.
Examiner's comments: The student has identified a relevant technique and has begun to explain a little of what its use reveals about the father. This could be improved by connecting it directly to how the speaker feels, rather than just talking about the father's character. The student should also consider why this feeling is repeated – what does the way the technique is used tell us about its importance?		**Examiner's comments:** The student shows they understand there are both explicit and implicit ideas within poetry and it's important to consider both. Not every line will be understood in an unseen poem – it is OK to occasionally offer a pair of possible interpretations. The student has tried to reach a reasoned judgement about the line they are unsure of, using further evidence from the poem, which shows critical ability.

> **REMEMBER**
> When you read a poem, always think about what ideas the poet is trying to convey through their writing.

> **REVISION TIP**
> Read the sample answers in this book carefully and try to understand why they are examples of lower- or high-level responses. Use this to assess your own work and see where you might make improvements.

Knowledge

7 Analysing one poem

Example 4

Feeling shown towards father: He was a generous and vibrant man.

Method/technique: Simile

> **LINK**
> Refresh your memory of simile on page 28.

Lower-level point	Example in poem	Higher-level point
The poet uses comparison to show she feels her dad was also a bit mad and liked cooking.	'He cooked like a person / dancing / in a yoga meditation'	Halfway through the poem, the speaker recalls a different side to her father. She shows she feels he was generous and good-natured through her use of a simile to describe how he cooked, 'dancing in a yoga meditation'. The image she creates is a strong contrast to his earlier seriousness and conveys that he was joyful yet also calm.
Examiner's comments: The student has made a simple observation. A quotation of a word or phrase would help improve this answer. It's also better to avoid colloquial expressions such as 'a bit mad' and express your ideas more formally. The technique category 'comparison' is correct. If you don't know the exact technique, it's better not to guess and just state what its effect is as this student has done.		**Examiner's comments:** The student shows awareness of the poem's structure while concentrating on one language technique. It is useful to think about where a technique is used in a poem, because this can have implications. Here it shows that a different part of the father's character is being explored by the speaker, and that reveals new feelings towards him, which creates contrast and depth.

> **REVISION TIP**
>
> Remember that poetry is lyrical writing, so 'hearing' the poem is as important as reading it. You may be able to hear techniques or rhythm that you don't immediately spot on the written page. Practise reading poems 'aloud' silently, in your head, during your revision.

Example 5

Feeling shown towards father: She is a positive person because of him.

Method/technique: Word choice: active verbs and metaphor

LINK
Refresh your memory of metaphor and verbs on pages 28 and 35.

Lower-level point	Example in poem	Higher-level point
The words 'dancing' and 'sharing' show the father enjoyed cooking. The words 'tossing' and 'seasoning' show the daughter enjoys cooking. This shows they are alike.	'dancing', 'sharing', 'tossing', 'seasoning'	The speaker shows she feels there is a strong positive connection between her father's actions and how she behaves now. When she describes his cooking style, she uses words that suggest generosity, 'dancing' and 'sharing'. Then, when she describes her own approach to life, she uses positive words, 'tossing' and 'seasoning', which are also cooking-themed. Through this metaphor, she shows she has been influenced by him, not just as a cook but as a person living life to the fullest.
Examiner's comments: The student has chosen good words to examine, but has misunderstood the cooking metaphor that is created in the speaker's behaviour. Make sure you carefully read the poem several times to try and avoid these kinds of error. Creating short, separate statements also makes it more difficult to connect ideas together. They could try using connectives such as 'as a result … however … therefore' to show how one example influences another.		**Examiner's comments:** This response shows how starting a point with the question focus (here, the speaker's feeling) then helps direct the flow of the point being made. The student examines one set of quotations, then the other, before bringing their meaning together. The concluding sentence considers the overall effect created and what the reader can draw from the imagery of the metaphor. It's important to show you understand how the poem is constructed to create deliberate effects.

Knowledge — EXAM

7 Analysing one poem

Sample answer 1: not a strong answer

Here is an extract from a student response to the question on page 44, with the examiner's annotations and final comments. It receives less than half marks.

> I really like how the poet has approached this poem because you know she must have been close to her father to write about him. **❶** The title got me thinking about her feelings. When you are getting old, you start thinking about it and often feel a bit down. **❷** So instead, Alice Walker wrote about her dad, who was also old but died. She shows she's sad about this when she says 'How I miss my father.' and then shows she feels that she shouldn't worry about feeling old because he had a good life and she thinks she's done alright too. **❸** Second, it's a bit odd but she never says she loves him. Nowhere in the poem does it use the word 'love'. So we know, she doesn't feel like she loves him, but she does say he taught her things, and at the end, she says he'd be proud of her. **❹** This shows that even though she didn't love him she respected him and he probably respected her, even if he didn't love her either. Because earlier it says he might have smacked her when she told the truth. **❺** In conclusion it doesn't seem like they had a great relationship, but her purpose was to show that you can still turn out alright whatever your parents are like. **❻**

❶ An opening statement can be useful, but it must focus on the question being asked. Whether you like the poem's approach or not is irrelevant.

❷ Good technique to consider, but the explanation is vague and assumes the examiner knows they are referring to 'Thirty-nine' as the age of the speaker.

❸ Correctly identifies that the speaker misses her father and that she is happy with who she has become, but there is guesswork about the poet's feelings about getting old, and the response wanders away from the speaker's feelings toward her father.

❹ An interesting observation, but does other evidence in the poem support the view? The absence of the word 'love' could just suggest they didn't express love by saying it aloud. Be careful about drawing absolute conclusions.

❺ The student has continued on a faulty line of reasoning and is drawing conclusions which are not supported by the poem's evidence.

❻ These ideas are unsupported and incorrect. A conclusion is optional, but needs to be accurate – and should not contradict any opening statement.

Examiner's comments

The student hasn't made any distinction between the poet and the voice of the poem. The student has identified some relevant feelings of the speaker but their explanation is often vague and lacks analysis – only one quotation is included. Few methods are examined, and one of those is a lack of a word. The student seems to be thinking as they write; as a result, one faulty conclusion leads them to make further statements which aren't supported by the poem itself.

Sample answer 2: a strong answer

Here is an extract from a student response to the question on page 44, with the examiner's annotations and final comments. It receives high marks.

① An opening statement that is connected to the question and summarises the student's overall impression. This might not gain marks in itself but it can help to focus an answer.

The voice in 'Poem at Thirty-nine' is a daughter reflecting on her relationship with her father and how much she learned from him to become the woman she is today. ① The title itself begins the meditative tone that is present throughout. Forty is a turning point in age for many people – 'Thirty-nine' suggests the speaker is contemplating her place in the world at this age before she moves into serious adulthood, but is doing it through the memories of her father and her feelings of appreciation for him. ② The first line explicitly says 'How I miss my father'. This is one of only three independent lines that are end-stopped with a full stop or exclamation mark. This emphasises their content is a significant feeling. This word 'how' also suggests he was very important to her and that his absence is something she feels very deeply. ③ We can infer that he was an important part of her life, and this is confirmed when she goes on to say she 'learned to see' he had 'escap[ed]' a difficult life. She implies she learned the importance of money from him by having a 'savings account' when she was still a teenager. ④ The second complete end-stopped line is 'He taught me how.' This is the second key feeling that the speaker shares: her father helped shape her as a person and she is grateful for this. ⑤ The poet helps build this feeling by structuring the poem into two distinct halves: ⑥ practical things she learned from him, then how his attitude to life influenced her.

continued

② Consideration of how tone is created, using contextual understanding to think about why the speaker might be thinking about her father and, importantly, how this affects her feelings towards him (the question focus).

③ Detailed focus on the effects of specific techniques and how these show the speaker's feelings.

④ Perceptive analysis shows the student has thought carefully about what is said and what can reasonably be inferred from the evidence in the poem. Good use of direct quotation to support ideas.

⑤ Clear response to the question focus.

⑥ Understanding of the poem as a construction, with correct use of subject terminology.

Knowledge EXAM

7 Analysing one poem

> There is far more creative language and imagery in the final three stanzas. This contributes to a cheerful atmosphere that celebrates her feelings for her father, particularly that his cooking brought him to life and gave others life. **She says he 'craved' the opportunity to share 'good food' and embellishes his craving with the word 'voluptuous'. This makes the image stand out to the reader and gives her emotion extra depth.** ❼

❼ Focus on language and imagery, shows insightful understanding and knowledge of effects.

Examiner's comments

This response is clear, well-organised, and full of critical analysis. The student uses plenty of direct quotation to help them analyse individual word choices, and also shows they understand the bigger structural elements stretching across a poem, such as tone and atmosphere. The student often uses the word 'feeling' or 'feels': this helps them stay focused on the question. Each point drives the response forward and explores the 'what', 'how', and 'why'. This ensures both assessment objectives are thoroughly covered.

EXAM TIP

Check over what you have written now and then to see if you are writing critically. Use these questions to help you:

- Are you stating what the poet's feeling, attitude, or idea is?
- Are you showing how the poet has presented their feeling, attitude, or idea?
- Are you thinking about why the poet has done this – what effect the method or technique has?

Retrieval 7

Answer the questions below. Cover the answers column with a piece of paper and write down as many answers as you can. Check and repeat.

Questions | Answers

1. How long should you spend on Question 27.1 in Section C: Unseen poetry? — About 30 minutes
2. How many marks is Question 27.1 worth? — 24 marks
3. How long should you spend on Question 27.2 in Section C: Unseen poetry? — About 15 minutes
4. How many marks is Question 27.2 worth? — 8 marks
5. How is Question 27.1 different from Question 27.2? — Question 27.1 focuses on one poem and expects you to understand and analyse meaning, as well as methods; Question 27.2 asks you to write about two poems
6. You should not use quotations from the poems in your responses. True or false? — False – you should use direct quotations and references to the poems to help support the points you are making
7. Put the strategy for analysing poem 1 into the correct order:
   - What stands out?
   - What does it mean?
   - What are your first impressions?

   Answer:
   - What are your first impressions?
   - What does it mean?
   - What stands out?
8. Why might it be helpful to try to 'hear' the poem by reading it in your head in the exam? — To help you recognise the rhythm and rhyme of the poem, and notice any words that are given particular emphasis
9. What is the goal of a second read-through of poem 1 when you are noticing and questioning? — To identify elements that might have meaning and to think about how the poem has been constructed
10. What is the goal of a third read-through of poem 1? — To evaluate and bring together ideas about meaning and reader response

Previous questions

Now go back and use these questions to check your knowledge of previous topics.

Questions | Answers

1. How does simile create comparison? — Simile helps the reader imagine that the things being compared share the same qualities
2. What is symbolism? — When an emotion or idea is represented through a symbol, such as an object, a person, a colour, or something from the natural world

Knowledge EXAM

8 Analysing two poems

Strategies

Question 27.2 has a much tighter focus than Question 27.1 and only tests AO2.

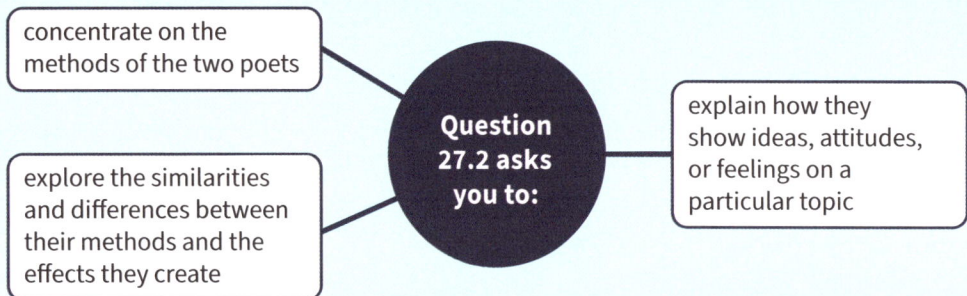

- Having already written your response to Question 27.1, you will be very familiar with poem 1 and the methods the speaker used to explore their ideas, feelings, or attitudes.
- A key part of the strategy for answering Question 27.2 is remembering your points about poem 1 as you analyse poem 2.
- Some ideas, feelings, or attitudes in poem 2 might naturally jump out as similar to or different from poem 1. You can then consider what methods are used to present them.

REMEMBER

Question 27.2 is only worth 8 marks, so try to focus on how the two poets create a specific idea, feeling, or attitude and comment on the methods used to do this. Think of Question 27.2 as exploring how poets may work differently to achieve a similar aim.

REVISION TIP

For Question 27.2, you only have about 15 minutes to read and analyse poem 2, compare it to poem 1, plan a response, and write your answer. During your revision, time yourself when answering practice questions and include your planning time. You might allow 5 minutes for reading and analysis, and 10 minutes for writing.

Example step-by-step analysis

1 Retrieve

Read the question and underline the focus. Briefly think about your analysis of poem 1 and what might be relevant to this focus.

2 Read

Read poem 2, holding the question focus in your mind. As you read, jot down:

- your gut reactions to the poem, such as its tone and how it makes you feel
- the feelings/attitudes/ideas it expresses that are relevant to the question focus
- anything you notice that is similar to or different from poem 1.

3 Identify methods

Read poem 2 again. You are now focusing on methods: look out for elements such as voice, tone, imagery, structure, comparison, and patterns, and note these down.

4 Compare and contrast to create a plan

Using your annotations/notes and your prior knowledge of poem 1, identify two, three, or four areas of comparison to write about. Each area should include:

- a point comparing how each poem shows the specific theme in the question
- quotations from, or clear references to, each poem
- a point comparing the method used in each poem
- a point that compares the effects of the methods.

5 Write your response

You do not need to write an opening or a conclusion, but you might find it helpful to begin with a point which allows you to comment on an overall similarity or difference between the poems. To achieve higher level marks you will need to link the methods used by the poets to wider ideas and meanings.

> **REVISION TIP**
>
> Write your own easy-to-remember key steps for your Question 27.2 strategy, to help you remember these in the exam.
>
> For example:
>
> - Read question; retrieve poem 1
> - Read poem 2
> - Consider what the poets' ideas are in relation to the task
> - Identify methods
> - Compare, contrast, and plan
> - Write response

Knowledge — EXAM

8 Analysing two poems

Sample analysis of poem 2

Below is a sample question and poem 2. The poem is annotated to show how a student has responded to it. This is stage 3 of the strategy on page 55: identify methods. A limited number of notes are shown, as in the exam, you will have little time for analysis.

The comparison poem 1, 'Poem at Thirty-nine', can be found on pages 42–43.

> In both 'Poem at Thirty-nine' and 'Those Winter Sundays', the speakers describe their feelings about their fathers. ❶
>
> What are the similarities and/or differences between the methods the poets use to present those feelings?
>
> [8 marks]

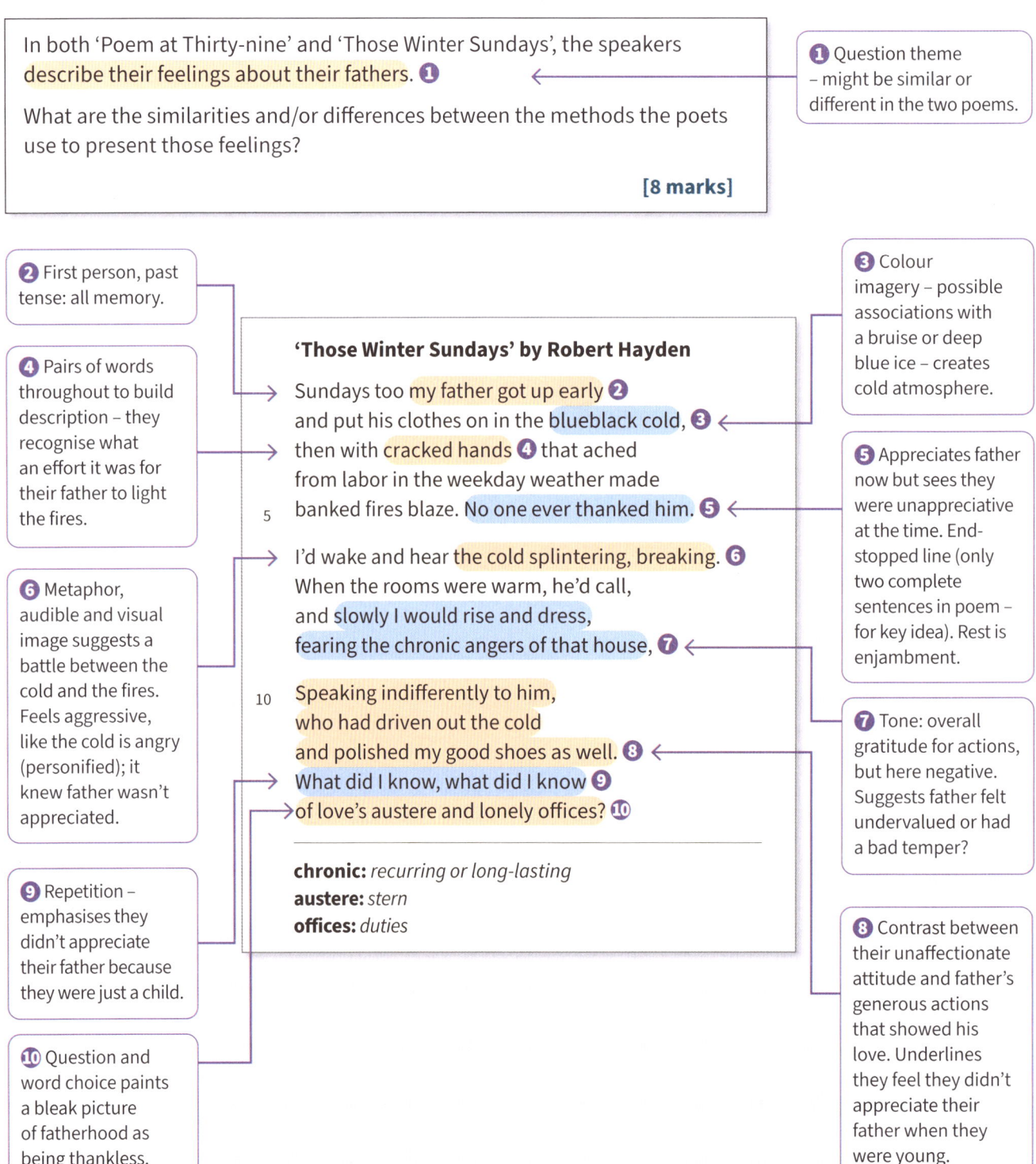

❶ Question theme – might be similar or different in the two poems.

❷ First person, past tense: all memory.

❸ Colour imagery – possible associations with a bruise or deep blue ice – creates cold atmosphere.

❹ Pairs of words throughout to build description – they recognise what an effort it was for their father to light the fires.

❺ Appreciates father now but sees they were unappreciative at the time. End-stopped line (only two complete sentences in poem – for key idea). Rest is enjambment.

'Those Winter Sundays' by Robert Hayden

Sundays too my father got up early ❷
and put his clothes on in the blueblack cold, ❸
then with cracked hands ❹ that ached
from labor in the weekday weather made
5   banked fires blaze. No one ever thanked him. ❺
I'd wake and hear the cold splintering, breaking. ❻
When the rooms were warm, he'd call,
and slowly I would rise and dress,
fearing the chronic angers of that house, ❼
10 Speaking indifferently to him,
who had driven out the cold
and polished my good shoes as well. ❽
What did I know, what did I know ❾
of love's austere and lonely offices? ❿

chronic: *recurring or long-lasting*
austere: *stern*
offices: *duties*

❻ Metaphor, audible and visual image suggests a battle between the cold and the fires. Feels aggressive, like the cold is angry (personified); it knew father wasn't appreciated.

❼ Tone: overall gratitude for actions, but here negative. Suggests father felt undervalued or had a bad temper?

❽ Contrast between their unaffectionate attitude and father's generous actions that showed his love. Underlines they feel they didn't appreciate their father when they were young.

❾ Repetition – emphasises they didn't appreciate their father because they were just a child.

❿ Question and word choice paints a bleak picture of fatherhood as being thankless.

Here are the student's notes for this question, following the strategy on page 55.

1 Retrieve

Feelings about their fathers

Poem 1: full of gratitude, practical lessons in filling in forms; nostalgic tone – misses him; generous nature that she's inherited; shaped her life – metaphor

2 Read

- Gut: full of regret, tone is sad, slow, and cold atmosphere
- Feelings: speaker remembers their dad doing kind things, enduring physical pain 'cracked hands', but everything the speaker did was wrong 'indifferently'
- Both appreciate dad, but poem 2 speaker didn't learn anything other than it's hard to be a parent 'lonely'. Both enjambed, like long, running memories

3 Identify methods

See notes on poem.

4 Compare and contrast to create a plan

Method: tone of speaker's voice Different methods, different effects, but similar theme	Poem 1 – grateful, nostalgic but uplifting 'he must have said'	Similar theme but presented differently: Poem 2 – grateful but guilt-ridden 'Speaking indifferently'
Method: imagery to show appreciation Different methods, different similar effect and idea	Poem 1 – uses simile and metaphor 'cooked … dancing'	Poem 2 – paired words, sensory language 'cracked hands'
Method: structure, mostly enjambment but end-stopped lines bring out important points Similar method, different effect and contrasting ideas	Poem 1 – what speaker learned, positive effect 'He taught me how.'	Poem 2 – what speaker didn't do, negative effect 'No one thanked'

8 Knowledge

Knowledge **EXAM**

8 Analysing two poems

How to write about two unseen poems

Once you have chosen the best areas to write up in your response, you need to focus on analysing the methods used, and how they link to the writer's ideas in relation to the question focus.

You could include:

- a point comparing how each poem reflects the question topic
- quotations from or clear references to each poem
- a point comparing the method used in each poem
- a point that compares the effects of the methods.

Here are examples of how some of the annotations on 'Those Winter Sundays' on page 56 could be written up into points in an exam answer. On the left is a lower-level response, and on the right is a higher-level response. The examiner's comments explain the strengths of each response and how improvements could be made.

> In both 'Poem at Thirty-nine' and 'Those Winter Sundays', the speakers describe their feelings about their fathers.
>
> What are the similarities and/or differences between the ways the poets use to present those feelings?
>
> **[8 marks]**

Example 1: Comparing how each poem shows the question topic

Poem 1 recalls a series of different moments that show the speaker was close to her father and appreciated him then and now. Poem 2 is fixed on one moment and shows feelings of belated appreciation.

Lower-level point	Higher-level point
In poem 1, she shows she appreciated her dad when she was young, and also when she was older. In poem 2, he only shows he appreciated his dad once he was a grown-up.	Both poems show feelings of appreciation for their fathers, but while the speaker in poem 1 recalls many special moments she shared with her father, the feelings shown by the speaker in poem 2 are much more complex. He is fixated on one point in his past when he was unable to appreciate his father and was ungrateful, but this is presented as a moment of adult recognition because he is reflecting on the events and can now see how much his father did for him.
Examiner's comments: The student does show a difference in feelings between the speakers, however this response could be improved by including thoughtful and insightful comments that show you don't just recognise the feelings, but can show how these link to writer's ideas and the question focus.	**Examiner's comments:** The student uses the wording of the question throughout: 'feelings shown', to keep their answer focused. They show understanding of the speaker's feelings in how they explain them ('special moments' for poem 1 and 'ungrateful', 'reflecting' for poem 2).

Example 2: Using quotations from, or clear references to, each poem

The speaker in poem 1 was close to her father and appreciated him as she was growing up. The speaker of poem 2 shows feelings of belated appreciation.

Lower-level point	Higher-level point
There are moments in the poems when there are clear feelings shown, for example: 'even in high school had a savings account' which shows the speaker was a nerd, compared to 'with cracked hands that ached from labor in the weekday weather made banked fires blaze' which builds a warm feeling.	We can see that the speaker in poem 1 responded to her father's guidance while she was growing up and appreciated its value because she had a savings account 'even in high school'. Similarly, now he is looking back, the speaker in poem 2 can see how 'banked fires blazed' through his father's efforts, showing his feelings of belated appreciation.
Examiner's comments: It isn't clear which poem each quotation comes from: always identify them in some way. There is brief, sometimes vague analysis of the effect of each quotation, and it does not all relate to the question focus of how the speakers felt about their fathers.	**Examiner's comments:** Appropriate and focused quotations from each poem are used in this answer. The student explores the similarity in what each quotation shows about the speaker's feelings and relates that back to the exam question.

Example 3: Comparing the method used in each poem

Tense and viewpoint:

- Viewpoint is first person in both poems.
- Only past tense in poem 2; both past and present tense in poem 1.

Lower-level point	Higher-level point
There is a similarity in the poems because both are written in the first person and both are written in past tense. Poem 1 also uses some present tense, which is a difference.	There is a similarity in the poems through the use of first-person perspective: both poems say 'my father' in their opening lines. Past tense in both poems emphasises these are poems of recollections, but the use of some present tense in poem 2 shows it is also a poem about growth and feeling grateful towards their father today.
Examiner's comments: The student makes a clear comparison. This could be improved by referring to the poem to show how the method is used, which would begin to demonstrate a higher level of understanding.	**Examiner's comments:** Methods are clearly identified. The student has referred to the poems by direct quotation. They then talk more broadly about a method in the poem and connect this to the question.

Knowledge — EXAM

8 Analysing two poems

Example 4: Comparing the effects of the methods

How different atmospheres are created:

- In poem 2, colour imagery compares cold to perhaps a bruise or deep blue ice – creates a cold atmosphere which shows the speaker had few positive feelings towards his father at the time.
- Poem 1 builds warm images of dancing, food, sharing, to reflect the feelings of warm respect and gratitude of the speaker.

Lower-level point	Higher-level point
Because the poets show their speakers' feelings differently, there are different methods in the poems. Poem 2 uses cold images and this is because the speaker was cold to his father and didn't appreciate him. But poem 1 uses warm images and this is because the speaker feels warmly towards her dad.	The poets show the speakers' feelings towards their fathers differently by building atmosphere through images. Coldness is created in poem 2 with 'blueblack cold', perhaps making the reader think of dense, solid ice. Consequently, the speaker's reaction in that cold place was thankless. In contrast, the speaker in poem 1 builds a warm and joyful atmosphere as her father is 'dancing' and 'sharing … good food'. This allows her to show her fondness for him.
Examiner's comments: The student is trying to think about the effects of warm/cold imagery but the comments feel disconnected and slightly back to front (cold images *create* and *reinforce* the effect that the speaker was cold to his father). Using phrases such as 'and the effect of this is …' can help you think about the impact of a method.	**Examiner's comments:** This student shows analysing effects means thinking about what *impact* the method has when it's used – what happens to the reader (here, they sense a cold atmosphere) and what happens to the speaker (here, the atmosphere colours their emotions).

> **REMEMBER**
>
> It doesn't matter how you refer to the poems, but you must make it clear which poem you are quoting from. You can say 'poem 1' or 'poem 2', or use the poet's name or the poem title. But be careful about using the poet's name – remember, the speaker is not always the poet, and it is important to recognise this.

8

Sample answer 1: not a strong answer

Here is a student response to the question on page 56, with the examiner's annotations and final comments. It receives less than half marks.

> Both the poems talk about the speakers' feeling towards their fathers. There are some similarities and some differences in the methods they use.
>
> The first method that is different is the tone of each poem. In poem 1 the poet is grateful and seems to like and appreciate her father ❶ 'This is the form, he must have said' ❷ and in poem 2 the poet is grateful but ashamed 'spoke indifferently'. ❸
>
> The second method that is different is how they build images. In poem 2 the poet uses pairs of words to create images like 'cracked hands'. In poem 1, the poet uses metaphor and simile 'He cooked like a person dancing'. ❹
>
> The third method that is the same is that they use only a few complete end-stopped lines, such as: 'He taught me how.' in poem 1 and 'No one ever thanked him.' in poem 2. ❺

❶ Simple comparison of the poems and identification of a relevant method.

❷ Precise choice of reference to evidence the method.

❸ Difference in tone identified and good direct quotation.

❹ Student uses same approach to identify another area of difference in method and provide evidence.

❺ Area of similarity across the poems identified.

Examiner's comments

This student has understood the need to identify methods and provide evidence from both poems, but needs to add ideas about the effects of each method in each poem.

REMEMBER

Remember, 'effect' can mean how the method creates meaning within the poem, and also how it creates meaning or inspires a response in you as the reader. This is why it's essential to think about how the poem makes you feel: your personal response is important.

REVISION TIP

Create a revision card of useful words to use for writing about effects. For example: 'emphasises', 'shows', 'implies', 'builds'.

8 Knowledge

Knowledge — EXAM

8 Analysing two poems

Sample answer 2: a strong answer

Here is a student response to the question on page 56, with the examiner's annotations and final comments. It receives high marks.

① This opening helps focus the response on the question: feelings about the fathers, different methods, and different feelings. It also identifies a difference and leads into a detailed comparison.

Both speakers in the poems are adults writing about their memories of their own fathers and conveying their particular feelings of appreciation of them. However, they express this appreciation using very different tones, which shows their different feelings. ① The speaker in poem 1 is remembering her father and how influential he was in her life in a grateful but nostalgic way 'This is the form, he must have said'. ② This effort to recall his actual words has the effect of showing how much the speaker appreciates him by remembering tiny details about how they interacted. ③

② A thoughtful point identifying a feeling and evidencing it with direct quotation.

③ An analytical comment on effect of the method.

④ The student uses connectives throughout to show clear contrast or similarity.

In contrast, ④ the speaker in poem 2 is full of remorse for how thoughtless he was as a child and how he spoke 'indifferently' to the man who'd made such an effort for him. ⑤ This makes the reader feel the father and son were not close, and that the speaker regrets that he couldn't appreciate what his father did at the time. ⑥

⑤ An insightful point from poem 2 comparing a different feeling and evidencing it with direct quotation.

⑥ A clear comment on the effect of the method.

Both poems use imagery to show what their fathers did that was special, but the ways imagery is created are very different. Poem 1 uses a simile to show the speaker appreciates her father's creative attitude to cooking: 'He cooked like a person dancing'. However, poem 2 uses pairs of words to build up harsh images of the struggles the speaker's father endured, ⑦ such as 'blueblack cold' and 'cracked hands'. This has a sensory effect for the reader who can

⑦ The vivid vocabulary used in this explanation contributes to a confident response and helps show how well the student understands the effects created by the poets.

62   8 Analysing two poems

feel the deep cold and the speaker's belated appreciation. There is a similarity in the way lines are structured in both poems. For the most part both poems are enjambed: both speakers are recalling moments from the past and the enjambment creates a feeling of hesitancy at times, or a rush, as though memories are alternatively difficult to remember or keen to be recalled. ⑧ Very few lines are complete and end-stopped, and this makes them significant. For example, in poem 1 the speaker says 'He taught me how.' and that perfectly expresses her thankful appreciation for him, but in poem 2 the end-stopped line 'No one ever thanked him.' is so poignant because it encapsulates the speaker's feeling that he just didn't appreciate his father as he should have done. ⑨

⑧ An analytical comparison of the method within the poems and the effects it has.

⑨ A further comment that builds on the use of enjambment and analyses, the effect of end-stopped lines, and how this connects to the shared topic of the speakers' feelings about their fathers.

Examiner's comments

This response is constantly analysing methods, effects, and feelings expressed within the poems. The student shows a clear understanding of the poet's methods and compares and evaluates their effects in creating meaning.

REVISION TIP

There is a lot to do in order to answer Question 27.2, but being able to analyse poems quickly and carefully is a skill that improves with practice. Use the practice questions and poems in this guide to help you.

Retrieval

Answer the questions below. Cover the answers column with a piece of paper and write down as many answers as you can. Check and repeat.

Questions	Answers
1. Question 27.2 only tests AO2. True or false?	True
2. How long should you spend on Question 27.2?	About 15 minutes
3. Which three of these might you be asked to compare? a) given statement; b) ideas; c) attitudes; d) theories; e) feelings; f) genres	b) ideas; c) attitudes; e) feelings
4. What should you 'retrieve' when you first look at Question 27.2?	Anything you can think of from your analysis of the poem in Question 27.1 that would be relevant to this focus
5. You must refer to the poems as 'poem 1' and 'poem 2' in your answer. True or false?	False – it doesn't matter how you refer to the poems as long as it is clear which poem you are referring to
6. When referring to the poem, you should only use direct quotations. True or false?	False – you can use quotations from, or clear references to, each poem
7. You should try to use long quotations in your response. True or false?	False – focusing on key words or short phrases can prompt you to write more insightfully than long quotations
8. When comparing effects, which of these should you do? a) summarise; b) state; c) analyse	c) analyse

Previous questions

Now go back and use these questions to check your knowledge of previous topics.

Questions	Answers
1. How long should you spend on Question 27.1 in Section C: Unseen poetry?	About 30 minutes
2. How many marks is Question 27.1 worth?	24 marks

8 Analysing two poems

Knowledge

9 Example 1: analysis of one poem

Analysing poem 1

You are now going to explore another sample analysis of poem 1 for Question 27.1.

Remember, the important stages of analysis include:

1 Respond: What are your first impressions?
- Who's speaking?
- What's the poem about?
- How does it make you feel?

2 Analyse: Think about
- the layout
- how the lines run on/stop
- the tone
- the genre/form
- the tense/voice
- any strong images
- rhyme/rhythm
- particular words
- patterns/contrasts.

3 Evaluate: What does it mean?
- What's the main message?
- What's the atmosphere/mood?
- What's the poem's purpose?

> **REMEMBER**
> - Question 27.1 is worth 24 marks so you should spend about 30 minutes on it.
> - The question asks you to focus on particular feelings, attitudes, or ideas in the poem.
> - You are expected to understand and analyse meaning, as well as methods.

> **REVISION TIP**
> When asked to focus on ideas, look out for:
> - points of view, speakers' opinions
> - abstract/philosophical ideas
> - hoped-for outcomes
> - actions/behaviours the reader might take or adopt.

Knowledge **EXAM**

9 Example 1: analysis of one poem

Sample analysis of poem 1

Below is a sample exam question and poem. A student has analysed the question and poem, using the suggested analysis questions on page 41. We have not shown every possible comment you could make on this poem, as in the exam you will have a limited time for analysis. You could try to find extra ideas or techniques you would choose to explore if answering this question.

> In 'New Every Morning', how does the poet present ideas about regret ❶?
>
> [24 marks]

❶ Question focus.

❷ Word choice 'New' suggests positivity, hopefulness.

❸ Positive statement, reinforces title and suggests that a new day is not something to regret. End-stopped line – suggests speaker feels strongly.

❹ Second-person address creates direct connection to reader.

❺ Regret is exhausting. Emotive and sensory word suggests physical exhaustion.

❻ Alliteration – sibilance adds to slow, exhausted feeling.

❼ Repetition of 'hope' and 'you'. Inclusive tone – the speaker includes themselves as needing hope; non-judgemental.

❽ Anaphora – 'Yesterday…' enforces the idea that regret belongs in the past because that's where things went wrong.

❾ Natural imagery of a harvest, biblical allusion of God as a protector, keeping the past and its regrets safe.

❿ Life is a balance of good and bad, both come and go. Rhyme 'glad, sad, bad', and alliteration 'bloom … blight'; antithesis 'fulness of sunshine/sorrowful night' (light/dark contrast).

'New ❷ Every Morning' by Susan Coolidge

Every morn is the world made new. ❸
You ❹ who are weary ❺ of sorrow and sinning, ❻
Here is a beautiful hope for you,—
A hope for me and a hope for you. ❼
5   All the past things are past and over;
The tasks are done and the tears are shed.
Yesterday's errors ❽ let yesterday cover; ❽
Yesterday's wounds, ❽ which smarted and bled,
Are healed with the healing which night has shed.
10 Yesterday now ❽ is a part of forever,
Bound up in a sheaf, which God holds tight, ❾
With glad days, and sad days, and bad days, which never
Shall visit us more with their bloom and their blight,
Their fulness of sunshine or sorrowful night. ❿

9

11 Commanding tone. Repetition of 'cannot' to show rejection of regret. Use of first person 'we' to include the speaker.

14 Metaphor to describe the sky's brightness as polished metal, appeals to visual sense?

17 Even though things may go wrong in the future, take strength from every new day and don't spend time regretting. Final line mirrors positive idea of opening line. Also repetition of 'sinning … sorrow' from line 2.

15 Let them go, since we cannot re-live them,
Cannot undo and cannot atone; **11**
God in his mercy receive, forgive them!
Only the new days are our own; **12**
To-day is ours, and to-day alone. **13**

20 Here are the skies all burnished brightly, **14**
Here is the spent earth all re-born,
Here are the tired limbs springing lightly **15**
To face the sun and to share with the morn
In the chrism of dew and the cool of dawn. **16**

25 Every day is a fresh beginning;
Listen, my soul, to the glad refrain,
And, spite of old sorrow and older sinning,
And puzzles forecasted and possible pain,
Take heart with the day, and begin again. **17**

sheaf: *a bundle of grain stalks tied together after harvest*
spent: *worn out/used*
chrism: *oil used to bless people and make them holy*
refrain: *an idea that is repeated*

12 Builds on earlier idea of God taking charge of the past, suggests humans can only control what they do today.

13 Structure: stanzas with fixed rhyme scheme stanzas 2–6 Gentle rhythm but formal structure suggests teaching, perhaps a lesson the poet wants to share?

15 Natural imagery and antithesis – placing positive image second makes those ideas stronger, suggesting hope is stronger than regret.

16 Holy, reflective imagery, implies every new day is a blessing.

9 Knowledge 67

Knowledge **EXAM**

9 Example 1: analysis of one poem

Writing about one poem

Once you have annotated the poem with your ideas, you need to choose the best ideas to write up in your response. Always read the exam question again before you make this choice.

Remember, there should be four parts to each point you make when answering Question 27.1:

- the idea, feeling, or attitude that is shown in the poem
- the method or technique the poet has used to show it
- the effect of the method or technique
- textual references from the poem.

> **REMEMBER**
> A perceptive point is one that goes beyond facts and basic observations. This is why it is best to think and plan before you start writing – time spent gathering your thoughts before you begin a response is time well spent.

> **REVISION TIP**
> As you gain confidence in the skill of analysis, try to work under stricter, timed conditions to help train yourself for the exam.

Beginning a sentence with 'The poet decides to…' or 'The poet uses…' alerts the examiner that you are focusing on an aspect of method. It shows that you are aware the writer has deliberately chosen to present ideas in a certain way.

On pages 69–73 are examples of how some of the annotations on 'New Every Morning' on pages 66–67 could be written up into points in an exam answer. On the left is a lower-level response, and on the right is a higher-level response. The examiner's comments explain the strengths of each response and how improvements could be made.

> In 'New Every Morning', how does the poet present ideas about regret?
>
> **[24 marks]**

Example 1

Ideas about regret: Regret is an exhausting emotion.

Method/technique: Emotive and sensory language

> **LINK**
> Refresh your memory of sibilance on page 27 and emotive and sensory language on pages 32–34.

Lower-level point	Example in poem	Higher-level point
The poet talks about being 'weary' which shows tiredness.	Use of emotive and sensory adjective 'weary'	The poet presents the idea that regret is an exhausting emotion by describing the reader as 'weary'. This word also suggests that they are physically hunched over and weighed down by regret. It's as if the speaker can see the reader, which helps connect them and makes the reader more likely to respond to the poet's message.
Examiner's comments: This is a very simple comment. When you are drawn to a particular word in a poem, ask yourself why the poet included it. The literal meaning is the first layer of understanding, but what is the implicit meaning? The hidden layers of meaning are essential to consider.		**Examiner's comments:** When writing about emotive or sensory vocabulary, you need to clearly identify the emotion created, give the words used to create that emotion, and explain why the word choice has this emotive or sensory effect. This student also considers how this affects the reader's response to the poem.

Method/technique: Sibilance

Lower-level point	Example in poem	Higher-level point
The letter 's' is being repeated in that line too which makes those words stand out to the reader.	Use of sibilance 'sorrow and sinning' to describe things that cause regret	The poet presents regret as a negative emotion. They describe the different things that can cause regret using words that create a tone of sadness: 'sorrow and sinning'. The use of sibilance emphasises the sadness, and also strengthens the slow, exhausted feeling created earlier in the line.
Examiner's comments: If you want to comment on particular words, it's always better to quote them so it's absolutely clear what you are referring to. 'Standing out' isn't a technique or an effect in itself – the student needs to explain why it matters that the reader notices them and how they affect the reader or the poem.		**Examiner's comments:** This answer is strong because it explains how one technique can have two effects. It's important to recognise that poets make decisions that are connected. These may be within a single line or across the whole poem. This student has thought about the wider impact of techniques, which is evidence of more critical thinking.

9 Knowledge 69

Knowledge — EXAM

9 Example 1: analysis of one poem

Example 2

Ideas about regret: Humans should not worry about the past as they can only influence the present.

Method/technique: Biblical allusion

Lower-level point	Example in poem	Higher-level point
The poem makes lots of references to God, which shows the poet is religious. This means the poem is all about being moral and behaving well. God punishes people who don't live good lives because we have free will and can choose what we do. So if we've got things to regret, it shows we've lived bad lives.	'God in his mercy receive, forgive them / Only the new days are our own'	There is a thread of biblical allusion running through the whole poem which helps the poet build the idea that the past is something beyond the power of humans. The poet suggests humans should not worry about the past, as they can only influence the present, when they say, 'Only the new days are our own'. This focuses the reader to think about what really lies within their own power: the things they can do today. Suggesting that God can 'forgive' the past shows the poet thinks the past is out of our control. We would need to be divine to change what's happened, so we should not spend our time trying to behave as gods, but as good people who change their behaviour today.
Examiner's comments: When you talk about allusion, you are showing your wider contextual understanding, but you can't talk about everything you know. Focus on what is *relevant* to the poem and the messages it is trying to share. This student is making general comments that aren't correct in the context of the poem, such as living good/bad lives. They need to focus on the poet's ideas on controlling the past – and what that shows about regret.		**Examiner's comments:** This student links points on how the poet uses allusion to show the reader their ideas about regret. This is essential – every point must talk about the method and link it to the question focus. To reach the higher levels, you have to show exploratory thinking. This student is exploring how the poet anticipates the reader should respond through their own actions, which shows consideration of the wider impact a poem can have.

LINK
Refresh your memory of allusion on page 10.

Example 3

Ideas about regret: Like the natural world, human life has seasons and is a balance of good times and bad times.

Method/technique: Natural imagery, comparison, and contrast

Lower-level point	Example in poem	Higher-level point
The poet makes lots of comparisons to nature so that we can think about it being similar to how we live. There are harvest comparisons as well as an image of 'bloom and blight'. This tells us that our life is like the natural world and we should learn from it.	'Yesterday now is a part of forever, / Bound up in a sheaf' 'bloom and their blight'	The poet has woven natural imagery and natural references throughout 'New Every Morning'. By doing this they create a clear parallel between the human world and the natural world that lives and breathes around us. They compare yesterday to the autumn harvest by describing it as bound in a 'sheaf' and talks of 'bloom' and 'blight', bringing to mind beautiful flowers yet rotting crops. Together these images show the reader that human life has both beauty and rot, and we have to bring in the harvest and store it away, whether it is good or bad. We can't regret one part of it – it's all important and part of life.
Examiner's comments: This answer presents the idea of natural imagery very simply. The student has some good ideas which could be developed further, and has included a relevant quotation, but the level of analysis is restricted. More 'what' and 'how' is needed: *What* does the harvest comparison mean? *How* does 'bloom and blight' tell us our life is like the natural world?		**Examiner's comments:** The student is exploring how a technique has been used across the poem to create a larger feeling and theme of the poem. Several quotations are embedded within the exploration of what the poet is doing. The effect of these together is then considered, and tied to the question focus in a very thoughtful piece of analysis.

> **LINK**
> Refresh your memory of imagery, comparison, and contrast on pages 28–29.

9 Example 1: analysis of one poem

Example 4

Ideas about regret: Humans need to be aware of getting caught up in regret, and should choose to accept what happens in life.

Method/technique: Structure – stanzas and rhyme pattern

Lower-level point	Example in poem	Higher-level point
There are 29 lines set in six stanzas in total, and the final five are the same length with the same rhyme pattern. Each stanza has a different idea so the poet's ideas are clearly set out by using stanzas.	Structure using stanzas and a regular rhyme pattern	Using a formal structure with mainly uniform stanza lengths and a regular rhyme pattern allows the poet to create a feeling that they are sharing important lessons about life and regret. Each stanza is focused on a different feeling or idea, for example stanza 2 talks about painful events that might cause regret as being part of yesterday, while stanza 5 pushes the reader to see what possibilities today can hold. The poet uses the stanzas as individual lessons to present their ideas clearly.
Examiner's comments: This answer doesn't tell us anything about how the structure helps the poet share their ideas, or how it contributes to the feeling of the poem or its purpose. The student has observed that one stanza is different, but hasn't asked why – for example, what function does that first stanza have in presenting ideas about regret? Just identifying a structural feature is not enough.		**Examiner's comments:** The student is commenting on the use of stanzas as a teaching tool – this contributes to the idea that the poet has a particular purpose and wants to instruct the reader about the best way to live life and avoid regret. The student has used the wording of the question to help keep their point focused, which can be a helpful thing to do in your response.

LINK
Refresh your memory of stanzas and rhyme on pages 19–21.

Example 5

Ideas about regret: Even though things may go wrong in the future, take strength from every new day and begin it with a positive attitude.

Method/technique: Structure – repetition/mirroring of ideas and words across stanzas

Lower-level point	Example in poem	Higher-level point
Mirroring is when the same words or the same ideas are used in different places in a poem. This poet has used it because they want the reader to think about the same thing at the start and end of the poem. Then they will keep it in their head after they have read the poem. For example in stanza 1 it says: 'You who are weary of sorrow and sinning' while in stanza 6 it says: 'And, spite of old sorrow and older sinning', which is mirroring and suggests regret.	Mirroring of ideas and words across opening and closing stanzas	The poet uses the opening stanza to set out their 'beautiful' hopeful message that every day is a 'world made new'. The closing stanza then mirrors this positive idea by describing every day as a 'fresh beginning'. The regretful ideas of 'sorrow and sinning' are mirrored in both stanzas as a reminder that bad things happen in life, but the reader should take strength from every new day and begin it with a positive attitude. Mirroring allows the poem to feel like it has come full circle, having taken the reader on a journey of inspiration. It also lifts the reader from being 'weary' in stanza 1 to 'take heart' in stanza 6 which reinforces the positive tone present throughout the poem.
Examiner's comments: You don't need to explain the meaning of any technique you comment on – the examiner will understand it. This student has some good ideas, but they lack depth when explaining them, and aren't linking their ideas together. The long quotations at the end don't add anything because they aren't analysed. The brief reference to 'regret' needs unpacking in more detail to explain what it tells us about the poet's ideas on regret.		**Examiner's comments:** The student has used frequent, short quotations from across both the first and last stanzas to evidence their ideas. Absorbing quotations into your points can help your writing flow more smoothly. The effect of the mirroring on the reader is clearly explained, as well as how it reinforces both tone and the poet's ideas.

Knowledge EXAM

9 Example 1: analysis of one poem

Sample answer 1: not a strong answer

Here is an extract from a student response to the question on page 68, with the examiner's annotations and final comments. It receives less than half marks.

❶ An attempt to identify a relevant idea, but the point is colloquial and rather vague.

❸ A relevant technique but a weak choice of vocabulary in 'good' and 'bad'. Positive/negative or cheerful/sad would show greater understanding.

❺ This explanation is disjointed from the previous sentence; using connectives can make points clearer and show greater understanding of method and effect.

> The poem has a lot of ideas about how you should live your life, like when the poet says that every day is new. It's kind of like living for today, which is a good rule to live by, except maybe then you don't learn from stuff you do wrong. ❶ So in this way I would disagree with her. ❷
>
> Secondly, she uses good words to talk about now and bad words to talk about what's happened before. ❸ So we know that she thinks the past is bad because it's all done: 'With glad days, and sad days, and bad days which never Shall visit us more'. ❹ Because they're not something that's coming back it means you can't change them so why worry? ❺ I agree with this – worrying doesn't make things better. ❻

❷ Whether they agree with the poet or not isn't part of this question: the student needs to concentrate on identifying the poet's ideas and methods.

❹ A long quotation and a simple point. Using the question wording 'regret' would help improve focus.

❻ Irrelevant comment, which also contradicts their earlier statement.

7 Adding specialist vocabulary to identify the tense or voice would improve this point.

Finally, the poet talks to you like you are listening, which is nice because you feel like she cares. **7** So even though she's really religious and religions are all about forgiving people, it does seem like she means it. **8** Her idea is that people shouldn't worry about forgiveness because that's God's job. That's not how I see it, but I do think that the poem suggests that there's a positive message in living for today not regretting stuff which is 'Every day is a fresh beginning'. So that's a hopeful idea. **9**

8 Confusing statement and there is no identification of the technique 'biblical allusion'.

9 Inaccurate inference made about 'God's plan'. There is some relevant detail about the poem's positive message, but this repeats an earlier comment.

Examiner's comments

The approach in this response is to discuss, rather than to analyse or explore. Only a few textual references are used and there is frequent vagueness or misunderstanding. While the Assessment Objectives look for a personal response, this does not mean sharing every idea you might have about the poem. Examiners are looking for engagement with and understanding of the poem's ideas, rather than your opinions.

No specialist vocabulary is used to identify methods and the student's own vocabulary choices are very limited. This implies a weak understanding of how the poet has constructed the poem and their ideas.

REMEMBER

Always write about 'the reader' instead of using the phrase 'I think …'.

EXAM TIP

A plan can help you avoid making meaningless points. It's a good idea to spend about 5 minutes planning, and refer back to your plan as you write.

REVISION TIP

When reading new poems, ask yourself: What do I think the poet means? How does that make me feel? Try to bring in these personal responses when you are explaining the effects of the poet's methods.

Knowledge — EXAM

9 Example 1: analysis of one poem

Sample answer 2: a strong answer

Here is an extract from a student response to the question on page 68, with the examiner's annotations and final comments. It receives high marks.

① Brief overview of the whole poem allows student to summarise the overall feeling and connect it to the question focus.

> In 'New Every Morning' Susan Coolidge presents incredibly positive ideas about moving on from regret in life. ①

③ Method identified, with precise choice of references from across the poem.

> One of the main ideas she conveys is that today is a wonderful gift which we should make the most of, rather than be being caught up in what went wrong yesterday. ② One way she shows this idea is through her choice of positive language. She chooses words such as 'new', 'beautiful', 'hope', 'healed', 'bloom', 'sunshine', 'brightly', and 'fresh'. ③ The reader then cannot help but make positive associations with the present day, which feels like a bright summer full of light, warmth, and possibility. ④

② Clear and relevant idea identified.

④ Thoughtful explanation of the effect of the method with reference to the reader.

⑤ Detailed exploration of how the same method is used for a contrasting effect and to present a different idea. Insightful understanding of purpose.

> In contrast, regret is described in melancholic and negative language: 'sorrow and sinning', 'tears', 'wounds', 'bled', 'blight', 'spent', and 'tired'. As a result, looking back and dwelling on the past is shown as an exhausting, painful, and futile process. The poet seems to be trying to convince the reader not to do this and to take her advice on living positively and well. ⑤
>
> Later on, the poet uses the metaphor 'the skies all burnished brightly' to describe today as a place that shines. She also uses antithesis such as 'tired limbs springing lightly' to suggest today is a place of energy and rejuvenation. Placing the positive image second in the antithesis has the effect of making it stronger, and therefore more memorable for the reader. We might then remember to focus on the positive elements of life rather than dwelling on regret. ⑥

⑥ Two different figurative language techniques explored, as well as an interrogation of how the antithesis was constructed for particular emphasis and purpose.

She writes alternately in the second person and the first person, which helps achieve her purpose of sharing her wisdom with the reader because it creates a close connection. When she is explaining that accepting what has happened in life means accepting you cannot change or undo it, she instructs the reader to 'Let them go' but then switches voice to include herself 'we cannot re-live them'. The reader feels like they are being drawn into a conversation, and reaching the conclusion with the speaker. This bond allows her ideas to become more acceptable. ❼

❼ Effects of the voices considered throughout paragraph and connected to purpose.

The poet also suggests that regret belongs in the past because that is where all the things that went wrong actually are. Using the technique of anaphora she repeats 'Yesterday…' four times to enforce this idea that the past should be allowed to 'cover' yesterday's 'wounds' and 'errors'. She brings in some biblical allusion to reinforce this idea and reassure us that God is taking care of it all – not just the things we regret but 'glad days, and sad days, and bad days'. The effect of this is a feeling that humans can also benefit from not dwelling on the happiness of yesterday. ❽ The poet presents the idea we have a responsibility to live well today and to 'face the sun'. ❾

❽ Insightful understanding of allusion, connected to the question focus.

❾ Concluding point which echoes the student's opening ideas.

Examiner's comments

This response is well-structured and moves through the poem methodically. A wide range of techniques are identified and explored, all well supported with precise quotations or clear referencing. The student links their points to the question focus and centres their discussion on the poet's ideas. They bring suggestions about purpose into their discussion of effects, which shows they are engaging with the poem itself and understand the different ways a reader might respond to, and be influenced by it.

EXAM TIP

The higher levels of the mark scheme expect you to be 'considering', 'analysing', and 'exploring'. An important part of this comes from how you show your response to the poem as a reader.

Retrieval

Answer the questions below. Cover the answers column with a piece of paper and write down as many answers as you can. Check and repeat.

Questions | Answers

	Questions	Answers
1	How long should you spend on Question 27.1 in Unseen poetry?	About 30 minutes
2	What three possible things might the Question 27.1 task ask you to focus on?	The poet's feelings, attitudes, or ideas towards a particular topic
3	Briefly summarise what you need to do in Question 27.1.	You need to identify the ideas, messages, and meanings within the poem that are connected to the task, and explore how these are created using different methods
4	Before you choose the points to write about in your response, it is a good idea to read the exam question again. True or false?	True – it will help keep you focused on what your points should be about

Previous questions

Now go back and use these questions to check your knowledge of previous topics.

	Questions	Answers
1	In the exam, you must try to find every possible meaning in a poem. True or false?	False
2	Which type of context might you use in analysing a poem in the exam?	General understanding about the world that you bring to the poem
3	What is the effect of writing in first-person perspective?	Events are told from one point of view and the reader shares the speaker's experience
4	How is the viewpoint of a poet shown in a poem?	Through the thoughts and ideas they express and in the ways they present them
5	What is a pause in a line between two phrases called?	A caesura
6	Why is the use of patterns across words, images, or ideas particularly important in free verse?	Because structure in free verse isn't generally created using methods of stanza, metre, and rhyme – instead it may be created through pattern
7	What kind of meaning is present in irony?	Implied meaning

9 Example 1: analysis of one poem

Knowledge

10 Example 1: analysis of two poems

Sample analysis of poem 2

You are now going to explore another sample analysis of two poems for Question 27.2.

Below is a sample exam question and poem. A student has analysed the question and poem using the strategy on page 55. We have not shown every possible comment you could make on this poem as in the exam, you will have a limited time for analysis.

The comparison poem 1 'New Every Morning' can be found on pages 66–67.

> In both 'Sympathy' and 'New Every Morning', the poets present **ideas about accepting what happens in life and moving forward.** ❶
>
> What are the similarities and/or differences between the methods the poets use to present those ideas?
>
> [8 marks]

❶ Question theme – might be similar or different in the two poems.

'Sympathy' by Emily Brontë

❷ There should be no despair for **you** ❸
While nightly stars are burning,
While evening pours its silent dew,
And sunshine gilds the morning. ❹
5   There should be no despair – **though tears
May flow down like a river:** ❺
Are not the best beloved of years
Around your heart for ever? ❻

They weep, you weep, it must be so; ❼
10 Winds sigh ❽ as you are sighing,
And **winter sheds its grief in snow** ❾
Where Autumn's leaves are lying: ❿
Yet, these revive, ⓫ and from their fate
Your fate cannot be parted,
15 Then, journey on, if not elate,
Still, never broken-hearted! ⓬

gilds: *covers in gold*   **elate:** *in high spirits*

❷ Poem has stanzas, regular rhyme scheme.

❸ Entirely second person – personal connection to reader.

❹ Similar use of imagery of day and night, but here it suggests time is constant and unchanging, and that's beautiful.

❺ Simile. Idea that by accepting grief and loss, we can avoid despair; different from poem 1 which says we should put grief and despair behind us.

❻ Rhetorical question. What has happened in the past can protect you as you move through life.

❼ Repetition. Grief is a part of life and should be expected and embraced.

❽ Personification. Poet uses natural world as example we should follow.

❾ Pathetic fallacy.

❿ Extended natural imagery across poem, showing time and seasons have a natural unchanging rhythm; we can learn from it by embracing what happens in life and moving on positively and hopefully.

⓫ Positive word choice. Idea that we get over loss; it's a part of life, like changing seasons, and we have to accept it.

⓬ Command/imperative. Similar idea and message to poem 1 – you must face the future positively.

Knowledge EXAM

10 Example 1: analysis of two poems

1 Retrieve

Ideas about accepting what happens in life and moving forward

Poem 1: positive attitude to moving forward in life, accepting that life is a balance of good and bad, the past cannot be controlled or changed so should be left in the past in order to move forward

2 Read

- Gut: positive, gently persuasive poem (poem 1 more rousing) but directs the reader to move forward in life positively
- Ideas: by accepting grief and loss, we can avoid despair; what has happened in the past can protect us as we move through life; grief is a part of life and should be expected and embraced; we get over loss, it's a part of life, like changing seasons, and we have to accept it; you must face the future positively and not allow past events to break you
- Both: natural imagery, second-person address, positive
- Different use of imagery: pathetic fallacy and personification vs antithesis and alliteration

3 Identify method

See notes on poem.

4 Compare and contrast to create a plan

Method: voice – second person Same method, same effect and idea though slightly different tone	Poem 1 – invigorating encouragement to approach life positively 'Here is a beautiful hope for you'	Poem 2 – gentle persuasion to approach life positively 'There should be no despair for you'
Method: rhyme and repetition Same methods, similar effect and idea	Poem 1 key ideas – good and bad things can happen in life, but they have to be accepted 'glad days, and sad days, and bad days'	Poem 2 key ideas – everyone faces bad times 'They weep, you weep'
Method: natural imagery through alliteration and pathetic fallacy Different methods, similar effect and idea	Poem 1 – alliteration to show feelings of despair and grief are universal across nature but are balanced so life can go on 'chrism of dew and cool of dawn'	Poem 2 – pathetic fallacy to show that the seasons reflect the pattern of grief and renewal 'winter sheds its grief in snow'

Writing about two poems

Once you have analysed the question and poem, you need to choose the best ideas to write up in your response.

You could include:

- how each poem shows the question topic
- quotations from or clear references to each poem
- the methods used in each poem
- the effects of the methods.

On pages 81–83 are examples of how some of the annotations on 'Sympathy' could be written up into points. The examiner's comments explain the strengths of each response and how improvements could be made.

> **REMEMBER**
> Always read the exam question again before you begin writing: it will help remind you of the shared topic of the poems.

> In both 'Sympathy' and 'New Every Morning', the poets present ideas about accepting what happens in life and moving forward.
>
> What are the similarities and/or differences between the methods the poets use to present those ideas? **[8 marks]**

Example 1: How each poem shows the question focus

Poem 2 suggests grief is a part of life and should be embraced in order to move on, while poem 1 suggests the past should just be put behind us and not dwelled upon.

Lower-level point	Higher-level point
Both poems think moving forward in life is important, but they have different ideas about how the past should be treated. As a result poem 2 makes the reader feel like the past can shape their future in a good way. Poem 1 makes the reader feel like the past is a burden.	Both poems present the idea that moving forward in life is important, but they have different ideas about how the past should be treated in order to move on successfully. Poem 2 encourages the reader to draw comfort from the memories of the past as an important part of moving forward. In contrast, poem 1 insists that we should let go of events from the past because overthinking them makes us worry about what we should have done differently, which stops us moving forward.
Examiner's comments: The student makes a clear comparison of an idea in the poems and comments on the differences between how they affect the reader, but these are quite simple observations. More analysis to connect the statements with what they show about the question focus itself would improve this answer.	**Examiner's comments:** The student summarises their overall point in a clear sentence, then goes back to examine each poem in turn. This can help you stay focused in your response because first you make your point of view clear to the examiner. Then you explain the effect on the reader each separate poet is creating.

Knowledge EXAM

10 Example 1: analysis of two poems

Example 2: Using quotations from or clear references to each poem

Poem 2 suggests grief is a part of life and should be embraced in order to move on, while poem 1 suggests the past should just be put behind us and not dwelled upon.

Lower-level point	Higher-level point
Poem 2 presents the idea that grief is part of life and also that the past as something that is essential. Poem 1 also acknowledges that bad things happen in life.	Poem 2 presents the idea that grief is part of life when comparing tears to a river because water is essential for life. Poem 1 also acknowledges that bad things happen in life, but by repeating words like 'cannot', the poet emphasises that the past should not be allowed to drag us down in the present. Instead, it should be let go.
Examiner's comments: Direct quotations or clear references should be used – this student only mentions the ideas in the poem, which is not enough to show they have understood *where* in the poem the ideas appear. A general statement to identify an idea is fine but you must go on to evidence it.	**Examiner's comments:** It is not always essential to quote from the text – this student shows how the ideas and meaning in the poem can also be clearly referenced by describing what the poem says. It's clear which parts of the poems they are discussing and that's what is important here.

Example 3: The method used in each poem

How imagery is used to portray grief and regret when accepting what happens in life: poem 1 uses sibilance and poem 2 uses personification.

Lower-level point	Higher-level point
The poems are similar in showing the idea that grief and regret are a part of life, but the poets use very different techniques to show this. Poem 1 shows it using the same letter in 'sorrow and sinning' to build an image of regret, while poem 2 shows it making the weather feel things. The connection with wind shows grief and sighing are natural things.	Both the poems show the idea that grief and regret are a sad and natural part of life, but the poets employ different techniques. Poem 1 uses the sibilance of 's' in 'sorrow and sinning' to build an image of sad, slow regret at past actions, while poem 2 uses personification in 'Winds sigh'. The connection with the wind emphasises the naturalness of grief, while 'sigh' is an evocative word that suggests both grief and the gentle sound of the wind itself.
Examiner's comments: The student describes techniques rather than naming them. Try to remember specialist terms and use them appropriately to show your understanding.	**Examiner's comments:** This student has used specialist terms in their answer, such as 'sibilance', but also words which help show they understand the images each poet is creating, such as 'sad', 'evocative', and 'gentle'. Doing this helps show the higher-level skill of 'insightful comparison'.

LINK
Refresh your memory of sibilance and personification on pages 27 and 30.

Example 4: The effects of the methods

How the same overall message that we should move forward positively in life is shown through imperatives in both poems.

Lower-level point	Higher-level point
Using imperatives means poets are trying to tell their reader what to do and feel. Poem 1 says 'Let them go … Take heart' and is often quite bossy. Its effect is to give the reader a bit of a shake-up about getting on with life. Poem 2 says 'journey on', but that's pretty much the only bit of telling off. The rest of the time they are quite gentle and persuasive that the reader should be getting on with life.	Both poems encourage the reader to move forward in life with positivity. This is partly achieved through their use of imperative statements such as 'Let them go … Take heart' in poem 1 and 'journey on' in poem 2. However the volume of imperatives in poem 1 far outweighs those in poem 2, which means the reader feels a constant urging from the poet to make the most of the present day. In poem 2, there is more subtle encouragement, but the use of an imperative in the final two lines is a clear message that carrying on, whatever life's difficulties, is essential.
Examiner's comments: This student has thought about how imperatives are used in each poem, but developing these ideas further would improve the answer.	**Examiner's comments:** This answer refers frequently to the reader, which helps them assess how they experience the poem and the effect of the chosen methods on them. The reader is a key part of understanding effect. A method may have a direct effect on the reader, by creating a particular atmosphere, for example, or an indirect effect, such as emphasising meaning which a reader will interpret.

> **REVISION TIP**
>
> Revising for unseen poetry isn't just about testing your knowledge and analysis of poetic methods. You should also take time to critically evaluate and improve your writing style so that your points are clear, analytical, and always relate to the question focus.

Knowledge

10 Example 1: analysis of two poems

Sample answer 1: not a strong answer

Here is a student response to the question on page 81, with the examiner's annotations and final comments. It receives less than half marks.

> The second-person voice is used in both 'Sympathy' and 'New Every Morning'. ❶ The reader can be closer to the poets because of this as they are talking straight to them. So this makes the messages of the poem easier to get through. ❷ It also has the effect of making the poems a bit like instruction manuals for life because they are telling the reader what to do. ❸
>
> There are comparisons in each of the poems so the poets can create images to share the poets' ideas. ❹ These ideas include that good and bad things can happen in life, and that we should just get on with life and accept the good and bad. ❺ There are lots of comparisons to nature, for example, 'winter sheds his grief in snow' (P2) ❻ and 'chrism of dew and cool of dawn' (P1). ❼ This has an effect of the natural world being important because we are part of it and it is part of us. ❽

❶ Beginning with the technique, rather than the idea of the poem can make it harder to focus on the question requirement.

❷ The student has begun to talk generally about the second person rather than focus on its effect in the poems.

❸ This point could be improved by giving examples of where the poets are giving directions to the reader, and explaining how they create an effect connected to moving forward in life.

❹ Relevant method used across the poems.

❺ Relevant idea is identified.

❻ The student switches between referencing the poems by title and 'P1'/'P2', which is a little messy.

❼ Relevant quotations chosen from each poem, but these need to be explained in more detail, perhaps by focusing on key words.

❽ The analysis of the effect is vague and isn't tied into the question focus.

Examiner's comments

It can really help clarify points if you begin by identifying what idea, feeling, or attitude is shown by the poem (or poems). A lot of the vagueness in this response stems from the lack of focus at the beginning of each paragraph. Think of the method as the 'how': this will be much clearer if you first explain the 'what'. In this response, the 'what' would be a relevant idea across the poems.

Sample answer 2: a strong answer

Here is a student response to the question on page 81, with the examiner's annotations and final comments. It receives high marks.

❶ Comparative statement that responds to the question focus.

Both 'Sympathy' and 'New Every Morning' present positive ideas about accepting what happens in life and moving forward. ❶ One way they do this is by addressing the reader directly using the second-person voice, which creates a closeness between the poets and their audience. ❷ This is particularly effective in 'Sympathy' when the poet says 'There should be no despair for you' because it shows the poet understands the reader will have faced troubles. The effect in 'New Every Morning' is slightly different because the poet is keener to lift the spirits of the reader. The statement 'Here is a beautiful hope for you' lifts the reader rather than commiserates with them. ❸

❷ Method and overall effect identified.

❸ Detailed, analytical comparison between the particular effects in each poem, using appropriate quotations.

The poems also both present the idea that good and bad things can happen in life, but they have to be accepted if we are to move on. 'Sympathy' uses repetition in 'They weep, you weep' which makes the reader realise they are not alone in feeling grief or upset: it's something that happens to everyone. Similarly, 'New Every Morning' uses rhyme and repetition to talk about 'glad days, and sad days, and bad days' and says 'we' cannot re-live them, good or bad. ❹
The poets want the readers to recognise that everyone has problems, but there is a solution. That solution is presented differently, though there is a similarity in the theme: both poems use frequent references to nature. ❺

❹ Embedded quotations help the flow of this explanation and accurate terminology is used to describe techniques.

❺ Similarity and difference are not always clear-cut – there may be an element of both, which is fine to explore.

Continued

Knowledge EXAM

10 Example 1: analysis of two poems

'Sympathy' uses the imagery of the natural world to show that feelings of despair and grief are universal, and to emphasise how important balance is in facing life's problems. ❻ There are references to day and night and to the changing seasons. Pathetic fallacy is used to suggest that the snow of winter is an expression of mourning: 'winter sheds his grief in snow'. This implies that the reader should also grieve but then 'revive' or recover. 'New Every Morning' uses double alliteration in 'chrism of dew and cool of dawn' to draw attention to the blessings of nature, and this image is also refreshing and suggests a new start ('dawn') in moving forward in life. ❼

❻ This statement connects back to question, helping the response stay focused.

❼ Perceptive analysis that shows understanding of theme and of how poets can use very different methods to achieve a similar effect.

Examiner's comments

This is a clearly-written response which compares a range of relevant methods. Identifying the idea at the start of each paragraph helps this student anchor their overall point before they move into detailed analysis of each poem. The quotations are well embedded, evidencing the chosen methods and effects successfully.

REVISION TIP

There is a great deal of concept knowledge at the beginning of this guide. When did you last read through it? Regularly flipping back to re-read and retest your knowledge will help embed the detail in your mind.

EXAM TIP

You can annotate the poems in the exam paper in any way that is useful to you. This includes underlining, highlighting, and writing notes and ideas.

Retrieval 10

Answer the questions below. Cover the answers column with a piece of paper and write down as many answers as you can. Check and repeat.

Questions / Answers

#	Question	Answer
1	How long should you spend on Question 27.2 in Unseen poetry?	About 15 minutes
2	How many poems do you comment on in Question 27.2?	Two poems
3	Which of these should you analyse in the poems? a) the ideas, feelings, or attitudes identified in the question b) the methods the poets use c) both	c) both
4	Commenting on the effects of the writer's methods to create meanings is not necessary. True or false?	False
5	What should you 'retrieve' when you first look at Question 27.2?	Anything from your analysis of the poem in Question 27.1 that would be relevant to this focus

Previous questions

Now go back and use these questions to check your knowledge of previous topics.

Questions / Answers

#	Question	Answer
1	Which of these shows allusion? a) 'Tik Tok Tik Tok goes the teenage clock.' b) 'O, my brother Bob is a beautiful boy.'	a) 'Tik Tok Tik Tok goes the teenage clock' because it makes a reference to the well-known social media platform, while 'Bob' is an unknown figure
2	What genre of poem tells a story or recounts an event?	Narrative
3	What should you 'retrieve' when you first look at Question 27.2?	Anything you can immediately think of from your analysis of the poem in Question 27.1 that would be relevant to this focus
4	When comparing effects, which of these should you do? a) summarise; b) state; c) analyse	c) analyse
5	What is the difference between atmosphere and mood?	Atmosphere is the general feeling within a poem; mood comes from how the reader responds to the poem
6	What does a closed form of poetry mean?	It is a form that follows set patterns and typical genre conventions

Knowledge — EXAM

11 Example 2: analysis of one poem

Sample analysis of poem 1

You are now going to explore another analysis of poem 1 for Question 27.1. The question and poem have been annotated by a student using the suggested analysis questions on page 41.

We have not shown every possible comment you could make on this poem. You could try to find extra ideas or techniques you would choose to explore if answering this question.

> In 'Red Brocade', how does the poet present the speaker's attitudes towards other people? ❶
>
> [24 marks]

❶ Question focus.

❷ Begins with an Arab cultural proverb; 'used to' is reflective/nostalgic.

❸ You should not be afraid of strangers, as many people are today – you should offer them hospitality.

❹ Free verse; list of questions: we should show politeness and compassion to other human beings.

❺ Caring for strangers can mean they become friends. Positive word: 'good'.

❻ Thinks the Arab proverb is right and now the speaker acts on it. They talk to the reader as though they are the guest.

❼ Questions show the speaker's hospitality; connection to the Arab proverb which says to feed strangers.

❽ red = visual image
brocade = tactile luxury
pillow = comfort
the = special / the only one so given to guest; also the poem's title, emphasising its importance.

❾ Thinks: all the family should be involved in welcoming the guest. Word choice – 'serve'.

'Red Brocade' by Naomi Shihab Nye

The Arabs used to say, ❷
When a stranger appears at your door,
feed him for three days ❸
before asking who he is,
5 where he's come from,
where he's headed. ❹
That way, he'll have strength
enough to answer.
Or, by then you'll be
10 such good friends
you don't care. ❺

Let's go back to that. ❻
Rice? Pine nuts? ❼
Here, take the red brocade pillow. ❽
15 My child will serve water
to your horse. ❾

11

11 We don't hear the stranger's question, only the point of view of the speaker. First person, present tense throughout.

12 Idea: being busy is an illusion. 'Armor' = is hard.

15 Inclusive word (the rest of the poem has 'I').

16 Onomatopoeia: pleasing, irresistible sound.

No, I was not busy when you came!
I was not preparing to be busy. **11**
That's the armor everyone put on
20 to pretend they had a purpose
in the world. **12**

I refuse to be claimed. **13**
Your plate is waiting. **14**
We **15** will snip **16** fresh mint **17**
into your tea.

armor: *US spelling of the word 'armour'*
brocade: *a luxurious woven fabric, often made of silk*

13 End-stopped sentence shows they place friendship above the demands of everyday life – they honour honours the old customs.

14 Possessive 'your' makes the reader feel that they are part of the household, they have a place at the table.

17 Very few adjectives, so those included are special: 'fresh' suggests something vibrant and alive, like their new friendship.

REMEMBER
If a question asks you to concentrate on the speaker's attitudes, this means their point of view – the methods they use to show what they think or feel about the question topic.

REVISION TIP
Practise writing timed responses to all sections of Paper 2. It is important to be strict about moving on to the next section to allow enough time for full answers.

11 Knowledge

Knowledge • EXAM

11 Example 2: analysis of one poem

Writing about one poem

On pages 90–93 are examples of how some of the annotations on 'Red Brocade' could be written up into points in an exam answer. The examiner's comments explain the strengths of each response and how improvements could be made.

> In 'Red Brocade', how does the poet present the speaker's attitudes towards other people?
>
> [24 marks]

Example 1

Attitudes towards other people: We should show politeness and compassion to everyone – whether they are a friend or stranger.

Method/technique: Listing of questions

> **LINK**
> Refresh your memory of free verse on page 22.

Lower-level point	Example in poem	Higher-level point
The speaker wants us to know that there is a right way and a wrong way to behave and that just talking at people isn't really great. This is shown in listing 'asking who he is, where he's come from, where he's headed'. That's a lot for a person to take in so it's rude.	'feed him for three days before asking who he is, where he's come from, where he's headed'	The speaker presents an attitude of compassion and politeness towards the stranger by explaining how they should be treated as guests. The speaker lists questions you should not ask for the first three days of their visit, setting each one on a new line. This mimics the way we might often eagerly fire questions at people we've just met, which shows the reader how intrusive and wearying that kind of questioning is. Their attitude is that we should let them rest in peace and politely wait.
Examiner's comments: The student seems to understand the attitude of the speaker, but is a little vague in their explanation – using the question wording might help focus the point. They have identified a relevant technique but don't consider the effect in detail.		**Examiner's comments:** The student is exploring not only what the speaker says, but how it is presented on the page. The layout of a poem can help deepen the effect of a technique so you should try to remember to look critically at a poem while reading it. This is particularly important in free verse, like 'Red Brocade', which offers more opportunity to set out lines creatively.

Example 2

Attitudes towards other people: Friendship is something special that is good for us.

Method/technique: The few adjectives used in the poem

LINK

Refresh your memory of onomatopoeia (page 27), sensory language (pages 32–33), and word choice (pages 32–36).

Lower-level point	Example in poem	Higher-level point
The poet doesn't use many adjectives in the poem so when she does use 'good, red and fresh' they stick out and make us think about why she has chosen them.	'good' 'red' 'fresh'	The poet doesn't use many adjectives so when she does use them they stand out as significant and reflect the speaker's attitude that friendship is something special. For example, they talk about 'good' friends, the 'red' brocade pillow which is offered to the guest and 'fresh' mint that will be snipped into their tea. The use of 'fresh' is particularly effective because it creates an image of something that's vibrant and alive, like the new friendship that is growing between the speaker and the guest.
Examiner's comments: The phrase 'makes us think' is never enough to give as an effect. You must go on to give suggestions of what the reader is thinking about – such as the importance of friendship, or that friendship is valuable or special. When quoting separate words from different places, use an ellipsis (…) between them; otherwise it looks as if you are quoting a line which doesn't exist in the poem.		**Examiner's comments:** The student describes the use of the technique as 'significant' and the attitude shown as 'special'. Doing this helps show that the student understands the connection between technique and attitude: the 'how' that the question is looking for. Embedded quotations are used well: each has a little contextual detail from its position in the poem showing in each instance why the adjective is special and how it reveals the speaker's attitude to friendship.

Knowledge EXAM

11 Example 2: analysis of one poem

Method/technique: Onomatopoeia

Lower-level point	Example in poem	Higher-level point
The poet uses 'snip' which is onomatopoeia, to show how the speaker cuts the mint and the effect is the snippy noise it makes.	'snip'	Using the onomatopoeic 'snip' adds a layer of pleasing sound into the poem, which makes the image of the fresh mint tea richer. It has associations of pleasure – snipping something with sharp scissors can be irresistible – so it also suggests the speaker's attitude is that friendship is pleasing.
Examiner's comments: The student has mis-explained the 'effect'. This needs to be the effect of the use of onomatopoeia, not the sound effect it actually creates.		**Examiner's comments:** The student shows how a single word in a poem can have real impact: it has meaning, it adds sound, and it deepens the imagery of the words around it.

Example 3

Attitudes towards other people: The Arab custom of treating strangers with respect is something we should honour and keep alive today.

Method/technique: Structure – positioning the reader to involve them in the poem

> **LINK**
> Refresh your memory of using perspective to craft voice on page 14.

Lower-level point	Example in poem	Higher-level point
At first the poet is speaking and the reader is just listening, but then the poet is speaking more to the reader and that makes the reader more involved. This changes in the second stanza, after the custom has been explained but before the poet has started explaining how they are going to treat strangers who visit them. The effect draws the reader in and makes it all more personal to them.	'Let's go back to that.'	At the start of the second stanza the speaker announces that we should 'go back' to the Arab customs of hospitality they have just described. This shows they agree that strangers should be honoured and treated respectfully. The speaker says 'let's' so they include the reader in this, and from this moment on they speak directly to the reader as though we are the guest they are receiving, and who is being lavished with attention.
Examiner's comments: The student is explaining rather than analysing – the result is that this feels like a very lengthy pair of sentences where not a lot is actually said. Their answer would be improved by using vocabulary that is more varied and more precise than 'more'. Remember too that the poet may not be the speaker – try to distinguish between them, when the question asks you to think about the speaker's attitude.		**Examiner's comments:** The effect of the reader's position is well explained here. The word 'lavished' captures how the speaker is focused on their guest and demonstrates their attitude towards other people. The attitude itself is insightfully described, using 'honoured' and 'respectfully'. It is clear that the student understands what they are writing about and trying to show that in their own words. This is what raises the quality of their response.

Example 4

Attitudes towards other people: The Arab custom of treating strangers with respect is something we should honour and keep alive today.

Method/technique: Structure – end-stopped lines

Lower-level point	Example in poem	Higher-level point
End-stopped lines make bold statements about a poet's attitude. We can see this at the start of the last stanza and in six other places. In all these cases, the speaker shows they think strangers are as important as friends.	'I refuse to be claimed'	The speaker reinforces their attitude that the old customs for receiving strangers are important to honour by an end-stopped line: 'I refuse to be claimed.' The full stop in this structure makes their decision seem firm and emphatic, because they are consciously putting their foot down against the demands of the modern world in order to serve their guest.
Examiner's comments: Sometimes it's better to focus on a single example of a technique rather than trying to talk about all the instances across a poem. This student's comments have become too general. It would be more successful to begin with the attitude, next explain the technique and how it is used, and then focus on one example for detailed analysis.		**Examiner's comments:** It is perfectly acceptable to investigate how the same attitude of a speaker is shown in more than one way in a poem. This student has successfully carried on exploring the speaker's ideas for honouring strangers, by explaining how the construction of end-stopped lines reflects the speaker's attitude.

Example 5

Attitudes towards other people: Strangers can become friends and have a place at the table.

Method/technique: Inclusive/possessive voice

LINK
Refresh your memory of voice on pages 13–17.

Lower-level point	Example in poem	Higher-level point
By the end of the poem 'I' has become 'We' which shows the speaker has warm feelings towards the reader and wants them to feel welcome.	Using 'I', 'we' and 'your'	The speaker shows the attitude that strangers can become friends when, having used 'I' all the way to the final stanza of the poem, they suddenly draw the reader into the action with 'we' and declares 'Your' plate is waiting. This makes the reader feel they have a place at the table within the family, and creates a feeling of warm acceptance.
Examiner's comments: The student has picked a relevant technique from the poem, used neat quotations and made a simple observation. Linking this more closely to the question focus would strengthen the response.		**Examiner's comments:** The student clearly shows how the voice of the poem changes, and its effect. Further consideration of how 'you' is used could extend this response even further.

Knowledge EXAM

11 Example 2: analysis of one poem

Sample answer 1: not a strong answer

Here is an extract from a student response to the question on page 90, with the examiner's annotations and final comments. It receives less than half marks.

> Attitudes in the poem include: you should not be afraid of strangers, like many people are today – you should offer them hospitality; we should show politeness and compassion to other human beings; the red brocade pillow is special; all the family should be involved in welcoming guests; being busy is an illusion – welcoming a stranger and making friends with them is something really worth doing. ❶ Wide variety of methods including: proverbs 'The Arabs used to say…', questions 'Rice? Pine nuts?', a zoomed-in image 'the red brocade pillow', word choices 'serve' and point of view (first person, present tense, that doesn't allow us to hear the guest's point of view). ❷ Summary: The poet uses the proverb to show us a different culture and a different way of thinking about things. Then the speaker shows how you could follow its advice and what it would be like. ❸ The poem has a very welcoming feel and overall shows that serving others and treating strangers as friends is the most important thing to do in life. ❹

❶ A selection of perceptive ideas about the speaker's attitude, but these need to be explored individually. A brief introduction that introduces the overall attitude of the poem could help to focus the direction of the response.

❷ Good variety of methods and apt quotations, but these should accompany individual points of explanation on how attitudes towards other people are created and shown.

❸ This would be a perfect opportunity to comment on how the poem's structure creates meaning.

❹ This is a concise summary and would be a suitable conclusion to a fuller answer.

Examiner's comments

This response is more like a plan than a coherent answer. The student shows good understanding of the attitudes of the speaker in the poem, recognises the methods the poet has chosen, and is able to grasp the overall effect of the poem. However, by dividing up these elements, they have not demonstrated a well-structured argument, nor been able to analyse the elements and consider the effects of each method. The details given could have been transformed into an excellent response.

EXAM TIP

The student here may have run out of time for Section C: Unseen poetry by spending too long on Sections A and B. You must leave about a third of your time for Unseen poetry.

Sample answer 2: a strong answer

Here is an extract from a student response to the question on page 90, with the examiner's annotations and final comment. It receives high marks.

> The speaker in 'Red Brocade' is shown to believe strongly in looking after other people and welcoming strangers as though they are already friends. ❶ The poet begins with the speaker reflecting on an Arab proverb 'The Arabs used to say...' which creates a nostalgic feeling, and implies the speaker yearns for generous rules of hospitality for unexpected guests. ❷ When she later says 'Let's go back to that', her attitude that a person can become more generous by embracing the wisdom of their own heritage is further emphasised. ❸ In the second stanza the speaker demonstrates the courteous and thoughtful behaviour to strangers that she believes is important. ❹ She does this by involving the reader directly in the scene to try and make them comfortable. ❺ She asks questions, giving the reader a choice of food to take away their hunger, 'Rice? Pine nuts?'. Then she offers the reader 'the red brocade pillow', which is clearly special and would add to the reader's physical comfort. Finally, she insists her child will 'serve' the horse, lifting this burden from the reader. ❻ Together these have a really sensory effect: we can imagine the taste and smell of the pine nuts, feel the richness of the 'brocade' and the soft pillow, and see the bright red of the fabric. We might imagine running water and the gentle whinnying of the horse. The reader is drawn into the poem and connected to its ideas. ❼ The red brocade pillow is particularly important because it symbolises the generosity of hospitality. It stands out in the poem as the only coloured item and the most clearly

❶ Clear understanding that the speaker is a 'construct' and shown to believe things by the poet.

❷ Student has chosen to work through the poem step-by-step, which can help explore how the meaning builds up through a poem.

❸ Deepens the explanation by bringing in a later quotation and considering its additional meaning.

❹ Clear attitude identified.

❺ Clear summary of method.

❻ Details given, to expand on the summary, supported by apt quotations.

❼ Detailed and critical analysis of effect. Shows imaginative engagement with the poem and understanding of the poet's intentions.

Continued

Knowledge EXAM

11 Example 2: analysis of one poem

described element. By offering such a beautiful thing to the guest, it shows the speaker's attitude that strangers should be given the best of what we have. ❽ Our instinct might be to keep these for friends rather than strangers, but this comes back to the idea that after three days the stranger may have become a 'good friend'. ❾ Its use in the poem title emphasises its significance.

We only hear the voice of the speaker in the poem, but repetition of 'not … busy' in the speaker's answers to imaginary questions from their guest has a reassuring effect. It shows the speaker feels nothing is more important than caring for other people. ❿ The speaker suggests the idea of being busy is an illusion or 'armor'. Armour is usually used to protect people but here it is preventing them from connecting with others and creates a false feeling of 'purpose'. The hardness of armour contrasts with the softness of the red brocade pillow. This suggests the speaker feels people in 'armor' are missing out by failing to welcome people using the old traditions. ⓫

❽ Significant image from the poem explored and connected to attitude.

❾ Brings in own understanding of human behaviour and connects this to the question focus.

❿ Method, quotation, and attitude clearly identified.

⓫ Thoughtful analysis and exploration of layers of meaning.

Examiner's comments

This response presents a critical and thoughtful exploration of the poem. A number of attitudes are identified and well supported with a mixture of direct quotation and textual reference. Meaning is considered at both a literal and an implicit level, recognising the effect on the reader and exploring the poet's possible intentions for a wider message about engaging with other people, particularly strangers. The response is insightful, well organised, and well written.

REVISION TIP
Read the mark schemes that AQA publish to accompany each past paper. They set out what they expect to see in each level of an answer, and give you 'indicative content' (a list of content you could explore) for every question.

EXAM TIP
If you find you haven't left much time for Section C, there is still a chance to gain some marks:
- Identify the technique you feel most confident in writing about.
- Focus on an attitude, idea, or feeling, the method, an example and the effect.
- Try for a second point, but do leave some time to answer Question 27.2.

Retrieval 11

Answer the questions below. Cover the answers column with a piece of paper and write down as many answers as you can. Check and repeat.

Questions | Answers

#	Question	Answer
1	How many marks is Question 27.1 worth?	24 marks
2	How many poems do you comment on in Question 27.1?	One poem (the first one)
3	What are the four parts to each point you should include when answering Question 27.1?	• The idea, feeling, or attitude that is shown in the poem • The method or technique the poet has used to show it • The effect of the method or technique • Textual references from the poem
4	What does the speaker's 'attitudes' mean?	Their point of view – the methods they use to show what they think or feel about the question topic

Previous questions

Now go back and use these questions to check your knowledge of previous topics.

Questions | Answers

#	Question	Answer
1	Why might it be helpful to try to 'hear' the poem by reading it aloud in your head in the exam?	This can help you to recognise the rhythm and rhyme of the poem, and notice any words which are given particular emphasis
2	Give two examples of possible themes for a poem.	Answers could include: love; hate; desire; illness; war; peace; beauty; growing up; sadness
3	What is the effect of writing in second-person perspective?	Writing directly to the reader can create a more personal connection between poet and reader
4	What effect do contrasting emotions in a poem have on the story within it?	Presenting different emotions allows the story of the poem to have greater depth
5	Give two ways rhythm can be created in a poem.	Answers could include: rhyme scheme; syllable stress (metre); pattern; how lines flow from one to the next (enjambment and end-stopped)
6	What is a connotation?	An idea or a feeling that is often connected to or associated with a word or phrase, in addition to its main explicit meaning

Knowledge — EXAM

12 Example 2: analysis of two poems

Sample analysis of poem 2

You are now going to explore another sample analysis of two poems for Question 27.2. The question and poem 2 have been analysed and annotated by a student using the same suggested strategy from page 55. We have not shown every possible comment you could make on this poem, as in the exam, you will have a limited time for analysis.

The comparison poem 1 'Red Brocade' can be found on pages 88–89.

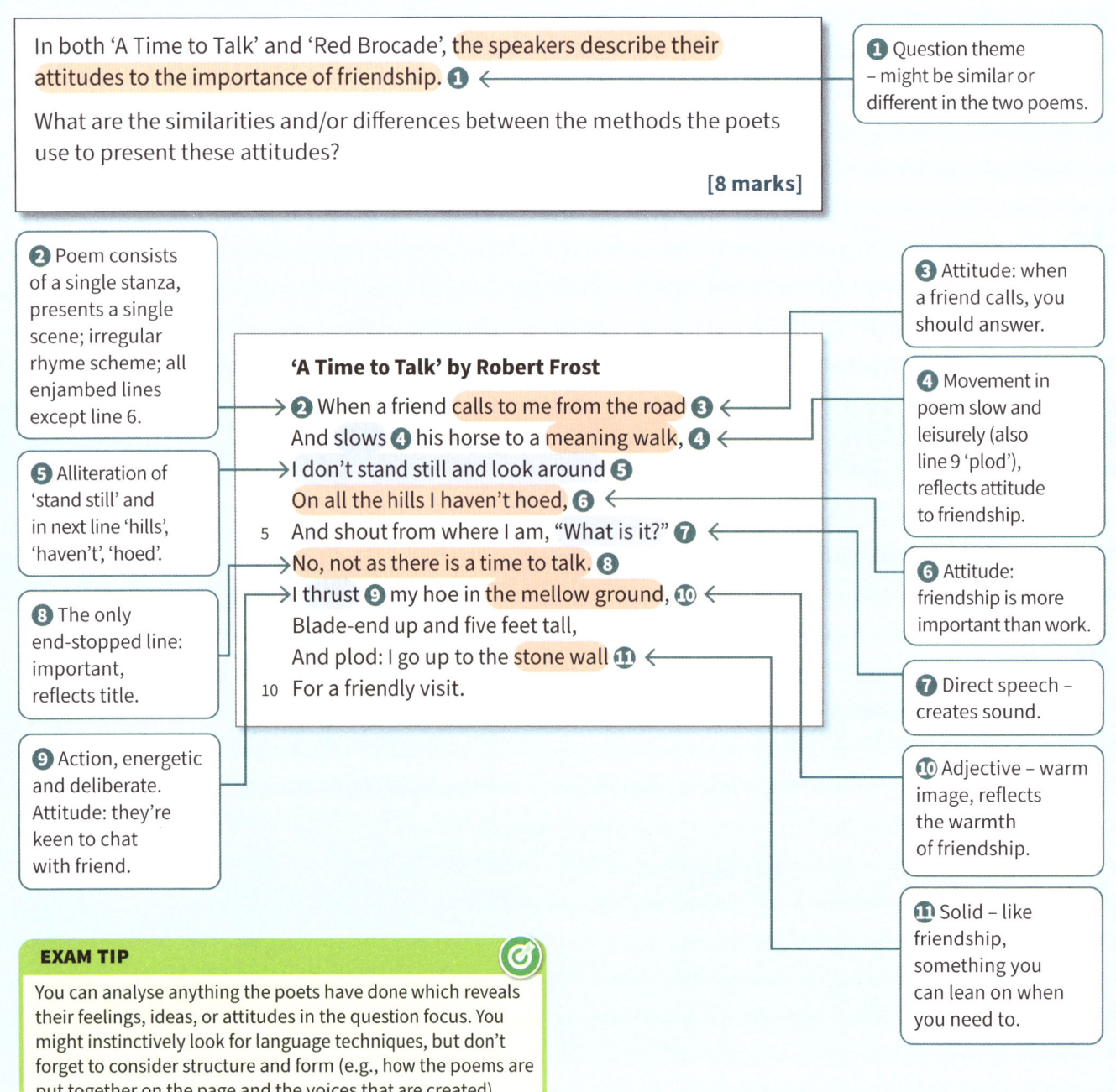

In both 'A Time to Talk' and 'Red Brocade', the speakers describe their attitudes to the importance of friendship. ❶

What are the similarities and/or differences between the methods the poets use to present these attitudes?

[8 marks]

❶ Question theme – might be similar or different in the two poems.

'A Time to Talk' by Robert Frost

When a friend calls to me from the road ❸
And slows ❹ his horse to a meaning walk, ❹
I don't stand still and look around ❺
On all the hills I haven't hoed, ❻
5 And shout from where I am, "What is it?" ❼
No, not as there is a time to talk. ❽
I thrust ❾ my hoe in the mellow ground, ❿
Blade-end up and five feet tall,
And plod: I go up to the stone wall ⓫
10 For a friendly visit.

❷ Poem consists of a single stanza, presents a single scene; irregular rhyme scheme; all enjambed lines except line 6.

❺ Alliteration of 'stand still' and in next line 'hills', 'haven't', 'hoed'.

❽ The only end-stopped line: important, reflects title.

❾ Action, energetic and deliberate. Attitude: they're keen to chat with friend.

❸ Attitude: when a friend calls, you should answer.

❹ Movement in poem slow and leisurely (also line 9 'plod'), reflects attitude to friendship.

❻ Attitude: friendship is more important than work.

❼ Direct speech – creates sound.

❿ Adjective – warm image, reflects the warmth of friendship.

⓫ Solid – like friendship, something you can lean on when you need to.

> **EXAM TIP**
> You can analyse anything the poets have done which reveals their feelings, ideas, or attitudes in the question focus. You might instinctively look for language techniques, but don't forget to consider structure and form (e.g., how the poems are put together on the page and the voices that are created).

1 Retrieve

Attitudes to the importance of friendship

Poem 1: strangers are people who can become friends if we care for them; you shouldn't be too busy to take care of friends; caring for new friends is something really worth doing; you should stand up for friendship

2 Read

- Gut: gentle moment in time, clear scene of one friend responding to another
- Attitudes: shows it's important to talk to friends, we ought to have the right priorities in life – taking time for a friend much more important than work
- Both: adjectives create mood, end-stopped lines
- Different: single scene poem 2, more ideas in poem 1; more energy in poem 1

3 Identify method

See notes on poem.

4 Compare and contrast to create a plan

Method: pace and energy Similar methods, different effects	Poem 1 key ideas – questions and directions show you should always be ready for strangers who may become friends 'Rice? Pine Nuts? / Here, take the red brocade pillow.'	Poem 2 key ideas – when a friend calls, you should answer, but there's no rush 'slows his horse to a meaning walk' 'plod'
Method: structure, focus on ideas Different methods, different similar effect	Poem 1 – several different ideas explored in different 'scenes' 'The Arabs used to say' 'No, I was not busy when you came!'	Poem 2 – action in single scene 'I go up to the stone wall / For a friendly visit'
Method: action and attitude Similar method, slightly different effect	Poem 1 – actions/imperatives show speaker is firm in beliefs 'take' 'I refuse' 'we will'	Poem 2 – moment of action reflects he's keen to chat with friend 'thrust my hoe […] blade-end up'

Knowledge

12 Example 2: analysis of two poems

Writing about two poems

Once you have analysed the question and poem, you need to choose the best ideas to write up in your response.

You could include:

- how each poem shows the question topic
- quotations from or clear references to each poem
- the methods used in each poem
- the effects of the methods.

On pages 100–103 are examples of how some of the annotations on 'A Time To Talk' could be written up into points in an exam answer. On the left is a lower-level response, and on the right is a higher-level response. The examiner's comments will explain the strengths of each response and how improvements could be made.

> **REMEMBER**
> Always read the exam question again before you begin writing: it will help remind you of the shared topic of the poems.

> In both 'A Time to Talk' and 'Red Brocade', the speakers describe their attitudes to the importance of friendship.
>
> What are the similarities and/or differences between the methods the poets use to present these attitudes?
>
> **[8 marks]**

Example 1: Comparing how each poem shows the question focus

Both speakers describe attitudes that show friendship is more important than everyday things such as work.

Lower-level point	Higher-level point
In poem 2, the speaker is busy working in his field when his friend stops by, so he stops to chat. In poem 1, the speaker remembers an old saying, then talks about how she would like to look after her friends, who are strangers at first but taking care of them makes them friends.	The importance of friendship is clearly presented by the speakers of both poems. In each poem, the speaker compares responding to the call of friendship to everyday burdens such as work (in poem 2) or general busyness (poem 1). Both speakers come to conclusion that friendship is far more valuable and worthwhile, and should be taken care over.
Examiner's comments: It can be easy to slip into describing what happens in the poems and forget to analyse them. This student has done that; consequently, there isn't a connection to the question focus. Adding phrases such as 'this shows that…' or 'therefore we can see their attitude is…' can help you avoid this mistake.	**Examiner's comments:** This student has made a focused comment comparing the similar attitude shown in the poems. They have identified how each poem shows this in its own way, then drawn them together again with a comparative conclusion on their mutual attitude.

Example 2: Using quotations from or clear references to each poem

Both speakers describe attitudes that show friendship is more important than everyday things such as work.

Lower-level point	Higher-level point
In poem 2, the speaker is busy working in his field when his 'friend' stops by for a 'friendly' visit, so we know he thinks friendship is more important than work. In poem 1, the speaker talks about how strangers become 'such good friends' once we take care of them.	The speaker in poem 2 demonstrates how important friendship is by first saying what he doesn't do when a friend calls – think about all the work he hasn't yet done: 'hills I haven't hoed'. The repetition suggests there's an uphill battle – lots still to do, but also makes it seem slightly absurd and therefore implies it's silly to worry about. Similarly, the speaker in poem 1 uses repetition to suggest people who 'pretend' to have 'purpose' by being too busy for friends are foolish and denying themselves something valuable.
Examiner's comments: Quotations which use the key word(s) from the question do not necessarily provide the best evidence. The student's choices here do not help them make insightful comments about the poet's attitude. They are evidence that friendship is a key theme of the poems, but that's not what you are being asked to explore – be critical about the evidence you select.	**Examiner's comments:** If there is more than one relevant comment to make about a quotation, then that should reassure you that it's a good one to include. This student is exploring the effect of the poet's method on a literal and implicit level. Both are tied in firmly to the question focus and don't wander off topic. The student uses several words with linked meanings to underline the similar effect in both poems: 'absurd', 'silly', and 'foolish'.

> **EXAM TIP**
>
> It is important to focus on *how* meaning is created through the effects of the poets' methods. Avoid comparing just the meanings in the poems – you will not gain marks for this.

Knowledge

12 Example 2: analysis of two poems

Example 3: Comparing the method used in each poem
Adjectives for mood: warm in poem 1 and vibrant in poem 2

Lower-level point

Language techniques help build mood, and the language in both poems here helps to do that. Overall, poem 1 is more energetic when it uses verbs like 'fresh', and poem 2 is gentler with words like 'mellow'. This shows difference between the poems, but the attitude is still the same that friendship is positive and important.

Examiner's comments: The student makes a relevant comment about language and mood and gives appropriate examples and quotations. A definite attitude is identified. It could be improved with more detail on the effects of the examples and what difference they show.

Higher-level point

There is a similarity in that the poems use adjectives to create mood and convey their positive attitude towards friendship; however, they create slightly different moods through specific word choices. Poem 2 describes the earth as 'mellow', suggesting a warm attitude that reflects the affection of a long-held friendship; poem 1 describes the mint for the tea as 'fresh', which is a much more vibrant choice and suggests an attitude of valuing new friendship.

Examiner's comments: The similarity of the method across the poems is clearly identified, as well as the different attitudes within each poem. This demonstrates how asking you to comment on similarities and differences between poems doesn't mean finding absolute likeness or contrast – there will often be shades of similarity or difference. Understanding them shows you have a more critical insight into the poems.

> **EXAM TIP**
>
> When deciding which methods to write about, focus on those you feel confident about. You may have learned the names of some obscure language techniques, but if you can't write in detail about how they help the poets achieve an effect, it's better to avoid them.

Example 4: Comparing the effects of the methods

How end-stopped lines are used to show strong attitudes towards friendship

Lower-level point

Both poems use end-stopped lines. While poem 2 wants us to feel that friendship is so special there's always time in the day for it, poem 1 wants us to feel like we should fight for friendship. You know an end-stopped line means something important about the question focus is being said, so we can see that both poems want us to pay attention at these points.

Examiner's comments: The student has made a simple connection between the effects of the method. They need to include more detailed comparison to move up the levels in the mark scheme. Never over-generalise about the way a poetic method can be used in a poem; methods rarely mean one thing only, so this could lead you to make errors when interpreting a poem.

Higher-level point

Poem 2 only uses one complete end-stopped line, in line 6, which makes its content significant, particularly as it is also mirrored in the title. It is evidence of the speaker's strongest attitude towards friendship that we should make time for it in our lives. The speaker in poem 1 also uses end-stopped lines to assert her attitude towards the importance of friendship firmly. For example 'I refuse to be claimed.' makes the reader feel the speaker is standing up for friendship.

Examiner's comments: The student gives a detailed explanation of the method used in poem 2, and how it highlights the attitude of the poet. The similarity in poem 1 is compared more briefly, but clearly considers its effect.

> **REVISION TIP**
>
> Choose one of the examples of Question 27.2 from this guide. Using the mark scheme, write a point which fits the Level 1 criteria. Then improve it to hit the Level 2 criteria, and so on, to Level 4. Sometimes seeing the difference across an answer can help you understand what it means to meet the higher-level criteria.

> **EXAM TIP**
>
> There are four levels in the mark scheme for Question 27.2: Simple, Clear, Thoughtful, and Critical. Keep these in mind as you are writing, to try to 'level up' what you are saying to reach the higher marks.

Knowledge EXAM

12 Example 2: analysis of two poems

Sample answer 1: not a strong answer

Here is a student response to the question on page 100, with the examiner's annotations and final comments. It receives less than half marks.

> Both the poems show the same attitude that friendship is a really important thing to look after. ❶ The poets create a different energy in each poem. 'Time to Talk' is really relaxed, shown by 'plod' while 'Red Brocade' is lively, shown by 'Rice? Pine Nuts? Here, take the red brocade pillow'. ❷ The effect in 'Time to Talk' is that the reader feels relaxed. This is different in 'Red Brocade' because the reader feels alive. ❸ The poems are structured differently. 'Time to Talk' is one stanza and 'Red Brocade' is four stanzas. 'Red Brocade' talks about different ideas and feelings so there is a lot going on and a reader feels part of that. But 'Time to Talk' only shows us one thing happening and because the speaker is talking about only what happens in that moment, the reader is just watching. ❹ There is a similarity in both poems having moments of action and energy. 'Time to Talk' just has one moment, 'I thrust my hoe', but it is a shorter poem. 'Red Brocade' has quite a few and the poet uses words like 'take', 'refuse' and 'will' to show the speaker's attitude. There is a similar effect from both poems in that we know the speakers feel that friendship is worth putting energy into. ❺

❶ Clear comparison between the poems.

❷ Consideration of the differences created in each poem. These examples could be analysed in greater detail to consider how the method creates these different energies.

❸ Clear difference identified in the effect of the method.

❹ Clear comment to identify difference and show consideration of the effect of the method on the reader. However, the statements are presented as short, disconnected sentences.

❺ This is a good connection of effect and meaning.

Examiner's comments

Ideas in this response are organised clearly and methodically, but to improve, some analysis needs to be added. While similarities and differences are identified, these could be more closely compared. Comparative vocabulary can help with this, as could adding a comparative sentence after an example from each poem. This could help the student bring their ideas together.

Sample answer 2: a strong answer

Here is a student response to the question on page 100, with the examiner's annotations and final comments. It receives high marks.

❶ Brief opening sentence to focus the response, noting similarity.

❷ Identifies difference and method.

❸ Critical comparison of poems and how the same method is executed differently within them. The effects of the method for the reader are analysed in detail.

❹ Clear comparison of method across the poems.

> Both the speakers in 'A Time To Talk' and 'Red Brocade' show the same attitude that friendship is a really important thing to nurture. ❶ However, they show there are different ways of caring for friends which are equally important. One way this is done is through the pace and energy of the poems. ❷ The speaker in 'A Time To Talk' shows that when a friend calls you should answer, but there is no sense of demand or haste. The poet creates a relaxed image when his friend 'slows his horse to a meaning walk', suggesting he's inclined to stop for a chat. The speaker responds by 'plod[ding]' up to him. The reader gets the sense that their friendship is easy and natural and something that's a well-established routine. In contrast the speaker in 'Red Brocade' is ready to spring into action should a stranger arrive, eager to turn that person into a friend. This is shown in the many offers of comfort they make 'Rice? Pine Nuts? Here, take the red brocade pillow'. We can imagine a guest being ushered in and plied with good things. It shows their attitude that a new friendship is exciting and needs different care. ❸ The poems are structured differently as 'A Time To Talk' only focuses on one moment when the speaker sees and goes to greet his friend, but 'Red Brocade' presents a series of moments: exploring the proverb, showing the treatment of the guest, and their interaction. ❹

Continued

Knowledge EXAM

12 Example 2: analysis of two poems

❺ Clear analysis of the effects of the structural method.

As a result 'A Time to Talk' feels like a little snapshot into the speaker's life, but 'Red Brocade' allows us to learn a great deal more about the speaker's philosophy on friends, strangers and modern life. ❺

❻ Connection of two methods: word choice and action, which allows the student to make insightful comparison. Clear commentary comparing the speakers' attitudes.

Although 'A Time to Talk' is much more relaxed, both poems do contain moments of action that reflect the attitudes of the speakers. The word choices in these moments are revealing. In 'A Time to Talk' the speaker shows one moment of real energy as he sets aside his tool: 'thrust my hoe … blade-end up'. This decisive action shows the reader he is keen to meet his friend and the shininess of the exposed blade is like a signal that he's on his way. There's more decisive action in 'Red Brocade' and the speaker uses imperatives such as 'take' and 'refuse' to show she is determined and firm in her approach to taking care of friends. Both poets' choices emphasise the speakers' attitudes that caring for friends is something really worth doing. ❻

Examiner's comments

This response demonstrates clear, high-quality analysis of the poems in relation to the question focus. There is constant evaluation of the effect of the methods identified. The student has chosen to talk first about poem 2, then poem 1, which works well in this particular answer.

EXAM TIP

For Question 27.2, time spent on a basic plan of methods and attitudes from each poem will help you stay on track as you write your answer.

REVISION TIP

There isn't 'one best way' to write a response, and sticking rigidly to PEE (point, evidence, explanation) paragraphs can limit your ability to write creatively about the poems. Try new ways of writing during revision to freshen up your response skills.

Retrieval

12

Answer the questions below. Cover the answers column with a piece of paper and write down as many answers as you can. Check and repeat.

Questions | Answers

1 How many marks is Question 27.2 worth?

8 marks

2 What are the five steps in the suggested strategy for answering Question 27.2?

1. Retrieve
2. Read
3. Identify methods
4. Compare and contrast to create a plan
5. Write your response

3 Why is it a good idea to read the exam question again before you begin writing?

It will help remind you of the shared topic of the poems

4 Which four elements might you include in each paragraph you write for Question 27.2?

- A point comparing how each poem shows the question topic
- Quotations from or clear references to each poem
- A point comparing the method used in each poem
- A point that analyses the effects of the methods

Previous questions

Now go back and use these questions to check your knowledge of previous topics.

Questions | Answers

1 How long should you spend on Question 27.1 in Section C: Unseen poetry?

About 30 minutes

2 How long should you spend on Question 27.2 in Section C: Unseen poetry?

About 15 minutes

3 Which three of these might you be asked to compare?
a) a given statement   d) theories
b) ideas   e) feelings
c) attitudes   f) genres

b) ideas; c) attitudes; e) feelings

4 Which two of these words or phrases would be useful in comparing the poems?
'however', 'in contrast', 'in conclusion'

'however', 'in contrast'

5 What is created through the repetition of sounds in words?

Rhyme

6 Why is sensory language an important part of building strong imagery?

Because it creates a close, physical connection between the reader and the ideas of the poem

12 Retrieval 107

Practice

Exam-style questions

Use the questions in this section to practise the knowledge and skills you have learned.

1a

> In 'Symptoms', how does the poet present the speaker's feelings about love?
>
> **[24 marks]**

> **'Symptoms' by Sophie Hannah**
>
> Although you have given me a stomach upset,
> Weak knees, a lurching heart, a fuzzy brain,
> A high-pitched laugh, a monumental phone bill,
> A feeling of unworthiness, sharp pain
> 5   When you are somewhere else, a guilty conscience,
> A longing, and a dread of what's in store,
> A pulse rate for the Guinness Book of Records –
> Life now is better than it was before.
>
> Although you have given me a raging temper,
> 10 Insomnia, a rising sense of panic,
> A hopeless challenge, bouts of introspection,
> Raw, bitten nails, a voice that's strangely manic,
> A selfish streak, a fear of isolation,
> A silly smile, lips that are chapped and sore,
> 15 A running joke, a risk, an inspiration –
> Life now is better than it was before.
>
> Although you have given me a premonition,
> Chattering teeth, a goal, a lot to lose,
> A granted wish, mixed motives, superstitions,
> 20 Hang-ups and headaches, fear of awful news,
> A bubble in my throat, a dare to swallow,
> A crack of light under a closing door,
> The crude, fantastic prospect of forever –
> Life now is better than it was before.

1b

In both 'I Saw You' and 'Symptoms', the speakers describe their feelings about love.

What are the similarities and/or differences between the methods the poets use to present those feelings?

[8 marks]

> **EXAM TIP**
>
> The higher levels of the mark scheme concentrate on quality and require you to show 'thoughtful' or 'insightful' comparison. A smaller number of areas that are thoroughly covered could earn the same or more marks as more areas that are only making simple points.

'I Saw You' by Joshua Henry Jones Jr

I saw you as I passed last night,
    Framed in a sky of gold;
And through the sun's fast paling light
    You seemed a queen of old,
5 Whose smile was light to all the world
    Against the crowding dark.
And in my soul a song there purled—
    Re-echoed by the lark.
I saw you as I passed last night,
10   Your tresses burnished gold,
While in your eyes a happy bright
    Gleam of your friendship told.
And I went singing on my way;
    On, on into the dark.
15 But in my heart still shone the day,
    And still—still sang the lark.

Practice

Practice

Exam-style questions

2a

In 'Dew', how does the poet present ideas about the power of nature?

[24 marks]

EXAM TIP

Always underline or highlight the main idea in the question to focus your mind before you read the poem.

'Dew' by Simon Armitage

The tense stand-off
of summer's end,
the touchy fuse-wire
of parched grass,
5   tapers of bulrush and reed,
any tree
a primed mortar
of tinder, one spark
enough to trigger
10 a march on the moor
by ranks of flame.

Dew enters the field
under cover of night,
tending the weary and sapped,
15 lifting its thimble of drink
to the lips of a leaf,
to the stoat's tongue,
trimming a length
of barbed-wire fence
20 with liquid gems, here
where bog-cotton
flags its surrender
or carries its torch
for the rain.

25 Then dawn, when sunrise
plants its fire-star
in each drop, ignites
each trembling eye.

2b

In both 'The Burning of the Leaves' and 'Dew', the poets present ideas about the power of the changing seasons.

What are the similarities and/or differences between the methods the poets use to present these ideas?

[8 marks]

> **EXAM TIP**
>
> Remember, you only have around 15 minutes for Question 27.2. You must explore the poem critically but quickly, to identify relevant methods to talk about.

From 'The Burning of the Leaves' by Laurence Binyon

Now is the time for the burning of the leaves.
They go to the fire; the nostril pricks with smoke
Wandering slowly into a weeping mist.
Brittle and blotched, ragged and rotten sheaves!
5 A flame seizes the smouldering ruin and bites
On stubborn stalks that crackle as they resist.

The last hollyhock's fallen tower is dust;
All the spices of June are a bitter reek,
All the extravagant riches spent and mean.
10 All burns! The reddest rose is a ghost;
Sparks whirl up, to expire in the mist: the wild
Fingers of fire are making corruption clean.

Practice

Exam-style questions

3a

In 'Countdown', how does the poet present the speaker's attitudes towards being a mother?

[24 marks]

> **'Countdown' by Grace Chua**
>
> After midnight, the tired astronaut
> surveys her chrometop kitchentop
> and counts the hours down
> till the alarm-clock rings.
> 5   Thinks of yesterday's shopping trip
> the kids outgrowing their shoes again
> and such unfinished things.
> Daytime, and her mother-ship
> shuttles its small satellites
> 10 from playschool to violin class,
> the swimming pool, art lessons, ballet,
> and feeds them at irregular intervals
> in a twenty-four-hour tour of duty.
>
> The washing machine groans. Pipes swish,
> 15 the dryer roars. She wishes
> she were in a vacuum,
> not vacuuming or doing dishes.
>
> She longs
> to be in the dark, and young,
> 20 with star-fields leaping light-years
> beyond time's gravity. And peers
> out of the window at the night,
> and counts down hours till the end,
> craning her neck, till all the clocks break free.

> **EXAM TIP**
>
> Some students like to read both poems and both questions before they begin answering Question 27.1, so they have a whole sense of the tasks together, which will always be connected by the poems' subject or theme.

3b

In both 'A Mother's Body' and 'Countdown', the speakers describe attitudes towards the sacrifices mothers make.

What are the similarities and/or differences between the methods the poets use to present these attitudes?

[8 marks]

EXAM TIP

Question 27.2 is the last question of the exam paper. If you find yourself short of time, try not to panic and remember that methods *and* effects are the key. Use those to guide your response.

'A Mother's Body' by Hollie McNish

if we watched their lips sing the same lullaby
they've sung a hundred times before
their arms cradle babies backs
in blankets made from pats and palms
5 we might realise how beautiful our mothers' bodies are

if we watched their thighs stride down streets
urging prams, praying toddlers sleep
or the tiptoes of their feet
sneaking in to tuck in kicked off sheets
10 when all their body longs for is one hot cup of tea
we might realise how beautiful a mother's skin can be

if we watched their backs gallop horses
round a thousand laughing playtime tracks
backbones arched in climbing frames
15 heaving tired piggy backs
we might realise the beauty that a mother's body has

and as day fades to night again; sunset teasing sleep
smiles hiding weeps because
they have not stopped for week on week
20 fingers flicking bedtime books as eyelids sink to sleep
lips leaned to foreheads
sealing children's dreams with last more kiss

we might realise how beautiful our mother's body is

Practice

Exam-style questions

4a

In 'Can't', how does the poet present the speaker's attitudes towards finding life difficult? **[24 marks]**

EXAM TIP

A poem's speaker can be the poet, or it can be a character. They might present attitudes towards the question topic that do not reflect your own point of view. Remember that you are not being asked to comment on whether you agree or disagree with the speaker, but to identify what their attitudes are.

'Can't' by Vikram Seth

I find I simply can't get out of bed.
I shiver and procrastinate and stare.
I'll press the reset button in my head.

I hate my work but I am in the red.
5 I'd quit it all if I could live on air.
I find I simply can't get out of bed.

My joints have rusted and my brain is lead.
I drank too much last night, but now I swear
I'll press the reset button in my head.

10 My love has gone. What do I have instead? –
Hot-water bottle, God and teddy bear.
I find I simply can't get out of bed.

The dreams I dreamt have filled my soul with dread.
The world is mad, there's darkness everywhere.
15 I'll press the reset button in my head.

Who'll kiss my tears away or earn my bread?
Who'll reach the clothes hung on that distant chair?
I must, I simply must get out of bed
And press that reset button in my head.

4b

In both 'Rain' and 'Can't', the speakers describe their attitudes towards facing life's struggles.

What are the similarities and/or differences between the methods the poets use to present those attitudes? **[8 marks]**

EXAM TIP

Once you've read Question 27.2, always think about what you already know about the first poem that is relevant. It's fine to reuse explanation of methods you used in Question 27.1, if it's relevant to this question.

'Rain' by Raymond Carver

Woke up this morning with
a terrific urge to lie in bed all day
and read. Fought against it for a minute.

Then looked out the window at the rain.
5   And gave over. Put myself entirely
in the keep of this rainy morning.

Would I live my life over again?
Make the same unforgivable mistakes?
Yes, given half a chance. Yes.

Great Clarendon Street, Oxford, OX2 6DP, United Kingdom

Oxford University Press is a department of the University of Oxford. It furthers the University's objective of excellence in research, scholarship, and education by publishing worldwide. Oxford is a registered trade mark of Oxford University Press in the UK and in certain other countries.

© Oxford University Press 2025

Written by Julia Naughton

Series editor: Lyndsay Bawden

The moral rights of the authors have been asserted

First published in 2025

All rights reserved. No part of this publication may be reproduced, stored in a retrieval system, transmitted, used for text and data mining, or used for training artificial intelligence, in any form or by any means, without the prior permission in writing of Oxford University Press, or as expressly permitted by law, by licence or under terms agreed with the appropriate reprographics rights organization. Enquiries concerning reproduction outside the scope of the above should be sent to the Rights Department, Oxford University Press, at the address above.

You must not circulate this work in any other form and you must impose this same condition on any acquirer

British Library Cataloguing in Publication Data

Data available

978-1-382-06758-4

978-1-382-06757-7 (ebook)

10 9 8 7 6 5 4 3 2 1

The manufacturing process conforms to the environmental regulations of the country of origin.

Printed in the UK by Bell & Bain.

The manufacturer's authorised representative in the EU for product safety is Oxford University Press España S.A. of el Parque Empresarial San Fernando de Henares, Avenida de Castilla, 2 – 28850 Madrid (www.oup.es/en or product.safety@oup.com). OUP España S.A. also acts as importer into Spain of products made by the manufacturer.

Acknowledgements

The author and the Publisher would like to thank Polly Coupar-Hennessy for her wonderful support and good humour as this book evolved.

The publisher would like to thank Jade Hickin and Sarah Cottinghatt for sharing their expertise and feedback in the development of this resource.

The publisher would like to thank the following for permissions to use copyright material:

Hafiz: 'My Brilliant Image', translated by Daniel Ladinsky from *I Heard God Laughing: Renderings of Hafiz* (Penguin, 1996), copyright © Daniel Ladinsky 1996. Reprinted by permission of the author.

Alfred Noyes: 'The Highwayman' from *The Highwayman* (Oxford University Press, 1999), copyright © The Estate of Alfred Noyes 1913. Reprinted by permission of The Society of Authors.

Alice Walker: 'Poem at Thirty-nine' from *Horses Make a Landscape Look More Beautiful* (HarperCollins Publishers, 1986), copyright © Alice Walker 1986. Reprinted by permission of The Joy Harris Literary Agency, Inc.

Robert Hayden: 'Those Winter Sundays' from *Collected Poems of Robert Hayden* (Liveright Publishing Corporation, 1985), copyright © Robert Hayden 1985. Reprinted by permission of W.W. Norton & Company, Inc.

Naomi Shihab Nye: 'Red Brocade' from *19 Varieties of Gazelle: Poems of the Middle East* (Greenwillow Books, 2005), copyright © Naomi Shihab Nye 2005.

Sophie Hannah: 'Symptoms' from *Marrying the Ugly Millionaire: New and Collected Poems* (Carcanet 28th May 2015), copyright © Sophie Hannah 2015. Reprinted by permission of Rogers, Coleridge & White.

Simon Armitage: 'Dew' from *Stanza Stones* (Enitharmon Press, 2013), copyright © Simon Armitage. Reprinted by permission of Morgan Green Creatives Ltd.

Grace Chua: 'Countdown' from *QLRS* Vol. 2 No. 4 Jul 2003, copyright © Grace Chua 2003. Reprinted by permission of the author.

Hollie McNish: 'A Mother's Body' from *Nobody Told Me: Poetry and Parenthood* (Blackfriars, 2018), copyright © Hollie McNish 2018. Reprinted with permission of Hachette UK Limited.

Vikram Seth: 'Can't' from *Summer Requiem: A Book of Poems* (Weidenfeld & Nicolson, 2015), copyright © Vikram Seth 2015. Reprinted by permission of David Godwin Associates Ltd.

Raymond Carver: 'Rain' from *All of Us: The Collected Poems* (Vintage, 1996), copyright © Raymond Carver 1996. Reprinted by permission of Wylie Agency.

Every effort has been made to contact copyright holders of material reproduced in this book. Any omissions will be rectified in subsequent printings if notice is given to the publisher.